CYBER TREK

By

S. Egroeg Reklaw

ISBN: 1-4033-0298-7 (Electronic)
ISBN: 1-4033-0299-5 (Softcover)

This book is printed on acid free paper.

1stBooks - rev. 5/24/02

CYBERTREK

Wait!

Mankin reconnected to Source for a spiritual connection away from the superficial and mechanically social morass with all the changing neurosis that presently surrounds him. He recalled earlier times in his life, living in the rural countryside where people sat, talked, and exchanged ideas without the ever-present watchfulness to be socially correct. There were no overburdened desires to be "politically correct" during those times. As he pictured in his mind's eye the slowly flowing stream, with limpid clear water, lush vegetation, and the voices of friendly people exchanging ideas on the numerous topics that affect their daily lives, he could still smell the ripening fruits—mangoes, tangerines, oranges, star apples, naseberries, and sour sops—that dotted the undulating hillsides. How could he ever forget the activity of the numerous species of bird that inhabited this terrain? They feed, nest, sing, mated and die as all living things do. All these things he remembered before he even knew there was the word *ecology*! He still smelled the sweet naturalness of the "fever grass" plant and recalled the pleasant taste of fever grass tea sweetened with wet sugar. Yes, wet sugar. He chuckled, as he realized how many things have changed, because the term *wet sugar* is not applicable in these times of mega-information and specific definition. Yes, read the label to determine your daily mega-dosage of vitamins! There, too, were tastes of other things not always pleasant. The taste of the dreaded ram-goat-dash-along tea was certainly a low time for anyone with any form of self-respect. One learnt early not to exhibit any form of sickness that would result in this form of dash-along medicine. Just remembering the taste of the tea, Mankin clenched his teeth, grimaced, and "time shifted" to the present complex and cybernetic time of faked perpetual smiles and its soulless bargaining just to make ends meet.

As the slow hum of the numerous workstations, personal computers, and other peripherals resonated about him, he wondered how can one be occupied like this for over a quarter-century, and actually retain one's humanity? He looked around for a measure of solace but found none. He knew, then, that he was here because he was trapped in a system that values things above humanity. He reasoned that if he was not yet destroyed, then it was time to get out. He would not stay in this type of cyborg environment, with its lack of spirituality. Psychologically, he knew how social systems could destroy the will of people. Mankin vividly remembered how the British "old boy" system fought to derail the Rastafarian movement in Jamaica in the 1950s and early 1960s. Those were the days when it was not fashionable to be called a Jah! Of course, Dreadlocks were not as ubiquitous as during the present time. Now, there are so many international "burn head wanna-bes," Dreadlocks masking as Rastafarians, that now it takes only a true Jah to define the Fakes. The Fake rank grows more numerous each day, as style and strategic planning for megabuck contracts, especially in the entertainment businesses, are determinants for their dress codes. As these pork-eating miscreants put on this shallow facade to rake in the money, one has to wonder; do they ever think about the origin of the Rastafarian movement or the meaning of the Dreadlocks. This question is directed to all people, not any special race, because some of the worst enemies of the Rastafarian's free expression were people of their own ilk. Church leaders you know who you are—you were then called "Pope Pious," and you were not even Catholic. You stood by unconscionably as the British paramilitary police force brutalized your brothers (and sisters) while you hid and counted your paltry offerings. Business as usual, "I am on the side of law and order. We cannot have chaos. Put the rabble in their place." Where is their place? Did you mean the prison where Marcus Garvey was warehoused because he spoke the truth? Sounds like whom…Pontius Pilate? Caiphas? Herod? This analogy is not comparing the persecution of Jesus the Christ by the Romans and the Jewish religious leaders of the day to the persecution of the Rastafarians by the Police and the Church, but "what I have written, I have written!" is the truth.

How can Mankin ever forget the first "true" Fake he met? He met this gentleman in San Francisco. Now, San Francisco is as international as any city can be. It has events that may make you shiver with fright, shiver with chilliness of spirit or temperature, shiver with unwillingness to participate, or take a quick exit to one of these Bible belt states. It is one of those low-crime, American big cities. There are many people sporting dreadlocks here, but they are not true Dreadlocks. Anyone can attest to the loneliness in these huge cities. It is overpowering, because you are in a jungle with the most ferocious predator: mankind. You are longing to meet a friendly face and heard your language spoken with the type of inflection that you grew up with. We all know there are English, and there are English, and then there are many more types of English accents. Imagine being very lonely and in a big city, watching a group of people in a crowd you believed are from your own country that you know will be glad to talk with you. You have to be specific here, because many of your own people may have no desire to talk with you. You could be from the wrong social class…and possibly, not their desired hue either! Anyway, you decided to introduce yourself. Your smile is not faked. You are a long way from home, but here is a little slice of home, at last.

"Hail I."

The retort; "I beg your pardon. Are you talking to me?"

Shocked! Mankin internalized himself, froze a smile on his face and politely mentioned he was wearing dreadlocks. Then came the big time response, "That's what they are called? Man, this style came from the Islands. Everybody wears them now." His womenfolk were so enamored by his hair; they continually played with it. Mankin shook his head and moved away, thinking about the old phrase, "getting absolute happiness by getting a lobotomy." Yes, it was understood that this "Locks One" was not making a radical statement of wearing his own natural hair in defiance of all the Western traditional values, which interprets the African appearance as odious. He was just being stylish, and possibly also, practicing practical economics to thwart the pomade manufacturers' and/or chemical makers' sale of their hair products. Humans dealt with disappointments in various ways, and Mankin's childish, immediate view was that this man previously used a hot comb in his hair, and we all know that heat is the enemy of the brain, so we can only expect him to be a bit silly. Then, disappointment has a tendency for us to externalize our biases and be hypercritical about trivialities. Playing back this event caused Mankin to redefine his stance on life and realize that some behavioral pattern in our youth cannot be effectively transferred to our latter years. Now, Mankin realized his error. The Locks One is doing his own thing, in his own culture, the way he knows how. At least he heard about the Dreadlocks and was willing to try it even though there were many detractors, and the trend was not having the great marketability that it enjoys today. Now, Mankin gave respect to the Locks-One who was willing to use his head to try something new, possibly before he even "sees the light" of his human naturalness.

With all these flashbacks in time, it was apparent that a physical shift was needed to alleviate the stressfulness of the present condition. In taking a journey over a quarter-century in time away from one's home it was apparent that there were opportunities lost and gained. Many times the equation of life did not balance in the sense of enjoyment. There were times when too many frustrations were relative to an increased quality of life. If you ever feel that frustration is overcoming the better qualities of life, then its time for a compensation shift. "You have been at the fair too long," as the old saying goes. As Mankin contemplated these things, he decided to talk with his old friend Willout, who he met in Toronto in the early days when things appeared so simple. The view then was that you get to North America and your problems would be solved. Looking back, now, it seems to Mankin that youth has a tendency to linearize all complex problems. The migrant's problems generally magnified after migration because they had shed old comfortable ways, and now, have major problems re-learning, and adjusting to new socially complex ideas. One of their mistakes is calculating the comparative relevancy of the quantity of dollars earned in their new country to the smaller amount earned in their native land. The belief that a greater quantity earned overseas will guarantee them a better sense of security and economic growth in their new land is a farce. There are hidden costs to this quantity, unlike the homeland of many immigrants where their homes are already paid for. Ever think your former homeland was perhaps a gentler and kinder place where family cooperation was at a premium but is now so artfully manipulated by the churches? Well!

"Willout, what do you think about moving to a kinder, gentler place?"

Willout answered, "Which 'bush' do you have in mind? Remember that type of slogan can cause political losses when you can't back up your words with action." It is true you cannot physically go back, but you cannot absolutely stay defocused and enjoy the "fair" either. As time passes, you have to make the compensating changes to keep up or be pushed aside as an observer. Time does not leave anyone behind; it carries one with it, unwillingly, outside the mainstream as an observer. To be left behind you would be in your own time and world to do your own thing. How can we presently define our focus? Are our past plans relevant today? Can we use our past plans to solve today's problems? Willout came up with the paradigm that we are still in the play, but there are too many changes in the place we usually call home. While listening to the discussion, Mankin also got the feeling from that the place called home was now inimical to their very existence. It could not guarantee the quality of life they grew accustomed to, or the personal security they came to expect, or the international renown their adopted country represented. The equating of the home country with buffoons was a little uneasy to bear. Perhaps there are too many intellectualizing and too little pragmatism. For many in the group, nostalgia was running wild. Some were still upset with the lack of opportunities during their youth, and others are just too unwilling to take a risk by visiting their former home. The latter group, one can understand. If you are a senior citizen, the risk you take with your meager resources may be your last. If it is your last resource, then you are lost. Or, to revisit the old village cliché, "Lawd, mi done!" —an old term used by the fore-parents during the years of the prolonged tuberculosis epidemic. When one is diagnosed with the disease one is immediately isolated from the population. "Lawd, mi done" was a physical place of rest and actually a state of mind. It was *end game* time for the sick, because they were on their final walk among the living. Enjoy their last sunset... "Lord, me done" with this world! End game time.

There are not many opportunities for advancement in the Third World (now, called developing countries) as the middle group should know. Mankin can still remember what the UK-trained Caribbean nurses purported to have told a minister of government when he tried recruiting them to return home. The gist was: "We were not qualified to be trained by you, but now that we are trained by the British, you want us to work for you. You could have all died out there for wants as far as we are concerned!" This group should remember that money is a tool, and what you do with it is your concern. The prime directive for the money tool is happiness. If you are happy where you are, then you have obtained Nirvana and possibly should stay there, although there are other altruistic points to life. The nurses had a good point when one thinks about the elitist structures operating in these islands during those days. They showed an unwillingness to have their own people trained by setting unrealistic entry standards that only a few students, the affluent types, could attain. On the other hand, many students who trained Overseas with government money refused to return and serve their country or even to repay their loans. For the government, it may be a dilemma, but its being repeated in the academic circles that most of these students got their loans through social or governmental connection. The grumbling among many overseas students is that the deserving ones without connections were never favorably considered for loans. It is no wonder there is no strong government incentive to collect on some of these student loans. People in the government, it seems, do not wish to hurt their friends and families. This type of continual government corruption comes back to kick ass. Even now, there are many recent horror stories on government's recruiting their own people overseas, and then reneging on promises made to returning immigrants where homes, transportation, and custom duties are concern. Is it that government can't deliver on their promises, or could it be that both parties failed to understand each other? Anyway, the greatest joke is the one where an island government sent a worker overseas to be trained. After graduation, a new government was sworn into office. This newly elected government refused continuing employing the trained student; telling him they were not the one who sent him on training! **Is this a joke?**

As Mankin perused the first group, he smiled with empathy as a fellow expatriate stared in the distance at make-believe houses, dotting the distant sloping hills. A reflective "foreigner," known as Simnally, quietly recollected on his youthful days. He envisioned the fading sunset on a cool evening while roaming along the sleepy and meandering Rio Cobre River. He could still smell the wood smoke from the numerous fires that mark the little houses as families prepared their evening meals. As he watched the billowing smokes spiral along the gray twilight hills, he tried guessing the level of readiness of each meal. He knew the darker smoke symbolized a fire that had been going for a long time, whereas a white abundance smoke meant the fire has just being lit! Here the food will not be ready for a while. With the final rush of animal activity before sunset, the birds, crickets, frog, and even the cows mooing in the distance added to the drama of cacophonic sounds to wave good-bye to the setting sun. His nose was teased by the local cuisine, which is generally a coconut-based meal of meat or fish or vegetables cooked in an abundance of thyme and eskellion. As he slowly walked along the winding hillside path in the dying sunset, Simnally could still smell the freshly turned earth, where farmers prepared to plant their crops. Friendly voices cooed, "Good evening" and invited him to dinner as he slowly made his way home. He tactfully accepted or rejected the invitations. He could still remember his faithful mongrel dog, Spot, jumping all over his feet in a warm welcome, bringing tears to his eyes. Those were the early, more slavish days. Now, he privately wondered within himself if he now got what he had asked for.

Someone called out, "Simnally, are you all right, man?" The older expatriate looked askance with yearning in his voice and slowly answered in a cool and controlled voice, "What are we really doing here at this stage of our lives?"

Mankin understands that this is the real world, not some laboratory tests where samples are taken to determine some extrapolated results. This is not some probability test here, it is real people having real concerns about their future to return to a country they love and would have liked to once again call home, although they believed this birthplace does not presently have their interests at heart. Still they fervently wish for positive changes that would give them an option as their aged bodies crave a familiar place of solitude. Now, their former home is a place seemingly run by foreign interests to make mega-bucks for the tourist industry. It is now a place where the environment is continually being destroyed to make another luxury hotel for the glorification of the local political nabob. A foreign island where inequities started to creep in as prime beaches escalated in price to make way for foreigners to play at the expenses of low-paid squatters. It is very difficult to identify with images of international criminal groups, where it seems the notoriety of the "criminal gunman" is the hero of the nation! Yes, the problem is understood, but to see some of these people taking credit at their jobs for coming from the same island as the Olympians, and in the same breath, decrying the islanders as groups of petty murderous criminals is too shameful. Refusing to return is one thing, but undermining your own "root" when it has never intentionally restricted your freedom is like "shedding your leaves" while marching onto a spiritual death of dis-connectedness.

Yes, Mankin learned something today about group dynamics from Willout and the rest of the expatriates in the US. In looking at the group, he wondered if his educated expatriate, Madhead, is actually better off than he was at home. He arrived here with tremendous scholarship cash, got his graduate and postgraduate degrees, but has never done any meaningful job in over ten years. His business acumen borders on the ridiculous. The poor fellow is still living in the British colonial past when things were static and well structured for the educated elite. This poor lost sheep is so devoured by the great American zest for competition that he started losing his reasoning. He failed to recognize that no form of advanced training would get him anywhere unless he applied himself to the American-type competition. He started to rationalize that the American security forces were spying on him to deny him employment. Everyone was laughing about this ridiculous suspicion, especially when he hinted that other people were using clandestine art in stopping him from getting jobs…this where everyone knew he was off track. He had been at the "fair" too long. Someone better enlighten him that we are strangers in a world where our family network is non-functional. Our uncles, aunts, and friends have no power here, neither are our local politicians—whether they are corrupt or benign! Unfortunately, there are many "spiritually" wounded migrants similar to Mr. Madhead and most are products of the North American illusion.

Looking over this group, and listening to various persons, Mankin recalled his Trinidadian friend Jah Wheels saying, "If you put the same effort in educating yourself in Trinidad, as you did in Toronto you would be long time better off." That seemed so long ago, but how true it is. It is really a fact that experience teaches wisdom. As Mankin listened to the discussion, it became plain that we were all longing for a quieter life. The plain fact is that the migrants were getting older and were quite concerned about retirements. They all had passed the days when Sound Systems blared out loud music in some dark dance halls or some other dimly lit *lawns*. A past time when hard misty bodies closely gyrated to the rhythms with heated breaths and pounding hearts tacitly inquiring how, when, and where after this dance! Those were the days, a very different time when transportation and hotel accommodations were at a premium for the (s)excited youths! Now, we all know that living in a small area magnifies gossips, especially among the older group of people who see themselves as being presently left out of the fun. (They possibly got "involved" too early, and now, have to stay home with their too-many kids. If you play early, you may have to pay later.) Someone here is passing this whole memory lane stuff off as *common* sense, where if you have that *certain* feeling without the hotel fee, then you will have...

"A feeling for the fields!"

This sounds so primitive and immoral to some now, but it was so predictable then. Was it considered wise then, definitely effective, or just purely we 'did it' our way! Excuses, excuses, excuses...to soothe an older mind. Mankin remembered being told that morality takes a vacation, especially when youthful emotions are at play. Who is chuckling with private youthful memory now? Share your experiences with us, if you dare! If our young ones only knew...what! Ever think how rigid morality seems to creep in as age advances and after you have come to believe that you had *done it* all? Is this satisfaction, selfishness, or an indication that your sensual potency is on the wane? No need to answer outwardly; *to thine own self be true*. No need to feel guilty, now, either; just remember that special discreet rendezvous...with inner joy...no it don't have to be in the fields, either, you big-city lunatic. But…feel the power of the fields. Country people rule! Ha.

Many Caribbean migrants have children who have grown up in North America. It is amazing how they all shared the common problem of fitting into a changing social order. For the Young Ones going to school, it was a frightful affair in not being able to speak with a North American accent; their parents generally could not either. These uneasy feelings were encouraged by biased teachers who believed all Black children are unable to learn academic subjects. Then there is the other stereotype—all Black people must be great athletes or entertainers. The teachers just used the United States' "Afro-model" for the Caribbean people, creating disastrous results for the children. Mankin heard horror stories in Canada of teachers turning a blind eye when migrant students were being picked on. In those days, in Canada, the local school bullies were mostly Italian. While the parents were being systematically pigeonholed, their children were fighting wars against unfeeling teachers who tried their best to rid their classes or schools of these strange alien children. Migrant students were then unfairly sent to trade schools by biased teachers, because the students were unable to participate in class discussions. There is a difference in tutoring in the Caribbean and the North American systems. In North America, students participate in the discussion. In the Caribbean there is generally no class discussion; the teacher lectures, and the students remain silent. One must remember that the teacher is not the only one at fault. The parents must bear the brunt of the blame. They generally abnegate their parental responsibility to visit the schools. When a teacher sent messages, parents often ignored them. Some would go to the teacher and act stupidly by suggesting the teacher should do whatever is considered necessary. The "whatever is considered necessary" is a parental suggestion to "go ahead, teacher, beat him or her into submission!" One teacher was heard loudly arguing with a mother who suggested corporal punishment. The teacher shouted, "How terrible! Are you mad?" When she mentioned calling the authorities, the frightened parent cringed with fright. At least give this trying mother credit for trying to solve her child's problem. Many other mothers just ignore these messages. One could hear many of these mothers bellowing in their well-furnished apartments (their only pride and joy) that they are not going to the schools, because if the child did not learn, it was the child's business. The outcome indicates that many times these children silently agreed with this assessment. On the downside of this parenting cycle the men all seem to be absent from the equation...possibly paying lip-service to the situation or listening to loud reggae music in some basement party with another "friend."

These parental types in the early days were just too unaware in making long-term decisions that affected their children. Most migrants were from a community where it is believed the institution knows best; a teacher's decision was generally left unchallenged. Over the years, these Younger Ones became the "new" North Americans. Presently there is a troubling feeling from the parents that something is terribly wrong in their family relationship. The parents no longer have the positive feeling of hope, which drove them in those earlier years. Even the Young Ones are now convinced that they will never be happy in North America, or in any of the European countries, especially in the United Kingdom. Could it be true, there is no place like home? If one does not believe, then check out the shift in European *ethnicity that is pervading all the European countries. Black foreigners are for the athletics programs only. Call them up during the Olympics and World Cup, wave the flags, have a good time, and then...?*

It must be remembered the migrants left their homes in the islands with great expectations of making a better life for their families and themselves. As the years went by this initial obligation has changed to one of pure survival by coping with the various forms of institutional racism and social stratification that are so rampant in these developed countries. Most immigrants to Canada can still remember when it was in vogue for almost every employer to ask, "Do you have Canadian experience?" If the applicant answered yes, the employer would then inquire how long had he been in Canada. The applicant knew if he said a couple of months, he would be disqualified for insufficient experience, and if he answered in the negative, he would be instantly and politely told the usual disqualifying response, "You have no Canadian experience."

One instance comes to mind of the unskilled Jamaican was told he could not be hired because he had no skill. He peeked into the warehouse and noticed the workers, mostly Italians, were packing boxes against a wall. When he asked if there were anymore vacancies for that type of job, he was told yes. He promptly applied for a job. Guess what? He was told he neither had Canadian experience or skill for that type of job! By this time, his Guyanese friend, Robert, who had accompanied him to the interview, was so enraged that he blurted out, "Can he come back for the job when he gets the approved color!" Of course, he was told that he was incorrect, and that color had nothing to do with it. Robert then applied for the job stating that he had a four-year college education, which he certainly did. He got the job with smiles from his employers. Robert then inquired the qualifications of his fellow workers and was informed they were either high school dropouts or semi-illiterate immigrants who could not speak English. He promptly told them he had no intention of ever working with their company, and the whole episode was a joke on their behalf.

It takes time for eventual realization to surface that we are out of synch with our society. We generally have so much trouble landing a reasonable job, and should you get one the avenue for promotion is generally nonexistent. It is reasonable to say our new environment is as hostile as walking in a war zone. Perhaps the best description was the one heard the from Mankin's radical friend, Simnally ("the Strokes") who got so annoyed with the low paying jobs in Toronto that he exclaimed, "These people have never heard that Lincoln freed the slaves." Simnally should have mentioned William Wilberforce and Clarkson, but he went totally North American...but that is all right, too! Mankin can remember the very first time he encountered the plastic appeasement smile. It happened at one of those government offices in Toronto just after a Provincial election. A well-dressed receptionist almost scared the clothes off his body when she stared at him with deep blue eyes, out of an attractively cosmetic-made face, and said, "May I help you, please." Then and there Mankin knew why most immigrants could not effectively cope in these foreign lands. They are not just devoid only of the social networks; they also have none of the ingrained superficiality that goes to make a "winner" in these lands. In a moment of desperation, all protocol was out the door, and there was a disembodied voice inquiring, "Why do you do that? You are such a pretty woman. You don't have to do that." The face behind the socially approved mask looked puzzled then professionally replied, "Do what?" Mankin put a body to the voice that said, "Smile the way you just did." The voice belonged to Mankin. The masked beauty replied in a calm and more humane voice, "I have to." Of course, the lady was correct. If she refused, the System would chastise her with social demerits, replace her with perhaps a newer and more compliant model, and then take her toys away... Miss Behaviorist could not allow that, so she chose not to misbehave! A very wise choice...it is extremely cold outside during the winter.

That was a moment of contemplation in Mankin's life. That simple incident caused a great amount of re-evaluation of the immigrants' behavior in the marketplace. The number one priority is to smile. Yes, paint a plastic smile on your face to appease everyone. If you are an immigrant looking for jobs in these environments, you will know how important it is to smile; not only to look pleasant, but also to keep on smiling. It is as if these people viewed foreigners as alien beings from another planet. Many times, while trying to let you feel welcome, they over do it by treating you as simpletons. Another thing is the false jocularity and the excesses of singling you out for help as if they heard you have a learning disability. The effect of all this contrived attention sometimes is the polarization of your coworkers in believing you are getting all the attention. They may be getting all the reasonable raises, as your boss may tell you that he had to spend more time training you because your skill level was lower than the rest. So, just be very careful of those special attentions. Everything is conditional and has its price, even friendship!

Simnally recalled the time he heard his manager telling some workers...

"If even the newly arrived people in Canada can understand this project, why can't you guys?" Are we to deduce from this that the laws of nature in North America are different from other places? Perhaps this narrow-minded manager has never heard that familiarity brings competence. These were the same workers who asked Simnally, "What are you doing here?" To which Simnally replied that he heard they were looking for his type of workers, so he applied and got the job, although this time *they* did not come with chains. A very simple reply and to the point, too.

Most travelers to industrial countries are generally motivated by economics. They generally equate higher wages with ease and comfort; a terrible mistake to make. This type of error has caused so many immigrants to put their lives on hold until they get enough money to realize their dreams. The dreams turned into nightmares as the decades went by, and their realities are lived in a cryogenic world, where their daily lives are continually postponed for a make-believe Utopian tomorrow. It is realistic to make plans for the future, but be aware that time is not linear, so you will not go from one point to another in a straight line. Your tomorrow may be now! Enjoy yourselves and not just by going to "basement parties." While you are at it, show some responsibility, too.

The rising sunrays dispersed the dotted white clouds that formed in the early morning over the multiple-peaked hills, while greeting us with such visual splendor. We wove our way through the hills, across the fields of wind generators with their spinning vanes, all configured in longitudinal and vertical directions to effectively trap the last watt of electricity from the cool draft that penetrates the cool hillside. Mankin watched the wind generators' motion against the background of the gray hill sides and conjured up thoughts of alien denizens from a distant planet, whose soul purpose is to exploit the Earth's resources and trap us all into a servile existence. As he reflected on this movie-motivated and a more like Star Wars-inspired thought, he compared this with the technocratic system where an idyllic neighborhood interfaced with that avaricious and populous technological monster known as the city, with its insatiable lust for more energy. Habitable neighborhoods are always losing their serenity to the jaded bureaucrats and their business-minded power lunch miscreants. As the old saying goes, "business people do not handshake, they interface." Yes, they have interfaced our humanity to oblivion.

As the low hum of the car motor and air-conditioner unit played their duet, Mankin wondered what this area was before all this power generation field was planted here. He was still enthralled with the innate beauty of the hillside, when one of his passengers, The Companion, broke the silence by tuning the radio to one of those stations playing mindless drivel about loving you absolutely. How do you love anyone absolutely? And why do these people glorify in these begging songs? If your love is an absolute for another, then where is the love for yourself? A bit tricky now because you have no leftover love for self—you gave it all away. Are you now having a loveless existence? Is it that simple? This is now too heavy to contemplate. This guy was promising to give things he could not possibly afford to give; they did not belong to him. The moon, the stars, and the sun are not his to give. These are celestial things. He then promised to give her everything he owns, perhaps this includes hate also. Mankin wonders how many relationships are built on these false premises where to utter the words "I love you" is an antidote to all ills. No one bothers to listen to the inner voice anymore; the visual stimulation by appearances, and the saying trendy in-things will pave the way. Mankin smiles, playfully thinking the singer may be a kind man, but he hopes the woman is just as kind. He hopes that when she gets them, she is willing to share the celestial bodies with others and won't leave the world in coldness and darkness because superficiality and mindlessness seems to be presently winning our Earthly game!

As the passionate friend, The Companion, stroked her cat and calmly mentioned how beautiful and romantic the song was, her fellow passenger; a world traveler from Guyana named Kat, asked, "Have you ever heard of Bob Marley?"

"Is he the one with the dreadlocks?"

"Yes," replied Kat.

"He does not sing romantic songs or make up his hair as our American artists do," replied The Companion.

"You mean he deals with reality and does not burn his hair to make it straight. Whatever gave you the idea that straight hair is better? Where does that idea come from, anyway?"

The Companion replied, "It looks better."

Kat looked at Mankin with disappointment, and mentally handed out demerits by shaking his head, sighing, and looking skyward as if asking for deliverance from the Creator for traveling with this undesirable animal. The journey continued for minutes in this type of pregnant silence when The Companion said, "You must agree that we Afro-American women are the prettiest in the world."

"Yes, you are physically beautiful, but such beauty has its downside, too"

"Everyone comes to America because we have what they want. Isn't it so, brother?" spat The Companion, with emphasis on the last word.

Mankin tacitly agreed, but he wished that this discussion would end. There were obvious frictions with his smooth talking Guyanese friend and the beautiful, but sometimes highly superficial, The Companion.

"You are right again," replied Kat.

The Companion turned around and glared at the stern-faced Guyanese, and challengingly inquired in a calm and mimicked educated tone, "Now, what is this I hear about beauty has its downside?'

Now, Kat is not one of those types you can easily push around and expect to compromise with later. This is one serious man from the Mackenzie area of Guyana who had traveled all over the world. On the other hand, The Companion, whose roots are from the mean streets of the East Oakland ghetto, is no compromiser either when it comes to women's issues, especially Black women. As Mankin observed the clash of the genders, he realized how cultures are playing the pivotal role in this confrontation. Neither of these combatants is really fighting along lines of race, gender, or social demarcation; they were fighting because of cultural unacceptability. The big question here is who will come to that realization first. Yes, we are Black, white, yellow, red, or whatever, but we are certainly not monolithic! We are individuals with our little local culture clocking in our heads.

The Companion continued with her voice a few octaves higher, bejeweled hands on her hips, her back erect and her neck going from side to side. There were no smiles this time; her well-applied blue eyeliner looked moist; her small mouth was pouted as she hissed through clenched, pearly white teeth: "You all come here trying to tell us what to do. Why doesn't your primitive ass stay where you were and leave us alone? You can't handle Black liberated women any way. Are your women sheep?"

Oh my gosh! This is getting dangerous.
"The downside of your beauty is that the majorities of you are simple and socially satisfied little creatures. You generally have no spiritual values to offer. Once past the

physical mask, there is nothing there. Your beauty is not even skin deep; it's painted on. In your world there is always a big can of grease and a bigger hot comb to soothe your pain," replied the man from Mackenzie with utmost disdain. Mankin could not allow this diatribe to continue much longer, because both parties were losing respect not just for each other, but they were losing respect also for Mankin himself. There were body languages and suggestive glances from both parties, querying Mankin's level of friendship and commitment to each individual. If this conflict should continue then Mankin would have to change his genus from mankind to mannequin. He then smiled at his own joke. At that moment he became aware of that The Companion was laterally looking at him, sensing his reaction to all the previous events. She obviously had no wish to show this combative side of herself, but competitiveness is synonymous with Americanism—first is first and second is nobody!

"You came to my house and abused me. Could I do that to you in your house, Mr. Foreigner?" asked The Companion, while she turned, and looked defiantly at her combatant in the rear seat of the car. Kat regained his composure and calmly replied, "Well, no, I have possibly gone too far. Look, let's talk about something else, please. You are a pretty, very polished, and highly intelligent woman, and our ancestors may have crossed the Middle Passage together at the same time, so please, let's save the fight for the common enemy."

"I am not expecting you to like me, just respect me for who I am."

"Lady, I have no disrespect for you. None whatsoever, but when you hinted that non-American women are a group of primitive sheep, you did us all a disservice. We just had a cultural conflict, and it was not nice. This conflict was about cultural definitions, not about race or genders. The USA is a great place to be at this time, and I hope our race can duplicate a nation like it. Our Black women outside your country are beautiful although they may not have access to the goods and services in the USA."

Mankin seized this opportunity to stop the conversation by adroitly steering the car at a sharp angle to the next lane. The Companion flew across the seat, pushing Mankin near the opposite door. She looked at him in a calm and suggestive animal way with wide beautiful brown eyes which lazily closed into small slits, then smiled and said in a low sensuous voice, "Would you have hurt me just to stop this conversation?"

Mankin answered in the negative and reaffirmed his belief that vibrating with the Cosmos is better than inflicting pain on another being, whether it be human or not. Of course, there are times when one has to deviate from this non-violence dogma. It's like saying we are all liberals until our interests are threatened! It really is funny how culture can play havoc with the human experience. Here we have two rational human beings that are considered well-centered and aware of the politics played by opposing groups. Yet they are willing to fight it out to a bitter end to prove that they are right. They each have the tools to tell them that each one is wrong, but the ego masked their good sense of reasoning. One has to ponder if this is attributed to culture or just personality traits in animals. Mankin's traveling companions proved how the meaning of words changed as we traveled through the different cultures. There are great misconceptions among people of African descents that we are all one people mentally, socially, philosophically, and psychologically, because we have the similar roots of one-hundred percent slavery in the Western World. This notion seems to be very prevalent also among the dominant race, which would generally say to an immigrant, "There is another 'guy' over there from your island also. You should go and speak with him." On checking out this guy, you may be surprised to find out the guy was born in Aberdeen, Scotland, and had never been to any of the islands except the British Isles. It is time to accept that people of the same color can have different personalities. The unfortunate part of this notion is that the immigrant population believed this myth and practiced it to their demise. Too many of us have the "crab in a barrel mentality" which tends to defeat us as a group. The institutionally advertised and socially reinforced notion that we as an immigrant group are all alike is so incorrect that sometimes one wonders how come it perpetuates itself. Simply, we gave the media the ammunition it needs to beat us down, by falling into many of the snares they constantly used to trap us. How about crime, social irresponsibility to the young, and a lack of maintaining contact with one's own homeland? In the euphoric moment of traveling from a depressed economy to the imagined Utopian industrial countries most immigrants believed they had it made, so they "'threw away their sticks before they finished climbing the hill" and stupidly severed all contact with their home base. This is a very costly error for any successful long-term strategy, because observation cannot be substituted for an actual physical experience. To see and to expect is not the same as to live through and to actually have the experience by touching…a kind of tactile touching experience at the keyboard (of life's experiences) as opposed to just watching others doing the work.

Mankin knew this great "expectation view" is fraught with errors and has caused tremendous problems with many immigrants. Where a person originates will generally shape his or her views. There are various levels of sophistication (and animal attributes, also) in all of us. Most times, we tend to resist changes that are beneficial, because to accept some of these changes is not just stressful going through the learning curve, but rejecting our old ways is like saying our beloved parents and respected teachers who taught us were wrong. In other words our whole society is inferior or wrong. Sounds reminiscent of how the European Overlords inculcated the whole African race so that their culture became dysfunctional, trivial, and worthless. My traveling companions had just showed a minute slice of the discord that permeates the immigrant society due to the dispersal of the Black race throughout various ruling colonial masters. It would appear that the most cohesive standard we have is skin color, which does not count for much if we should go by everyday occurrences. Just check out the internal strife (and murder) within the immigrant people of the same national group. It brings to mind the feeling that some of their business places, especially their dances, are invitations to the "dance" of death—a mirror image of upheavals in Africa (**African wars and tribalism)** according to people who are considered not so friendly to certain immigrant groups. They may not be friendly, but are their observations true? How pathetic. What about a sense of camaraderie among the various dispersed groups? We always hear a lot of verbiage about brotherhood (oops, sisterhood, too). Perhaps understanding takes a backseat to economic power...? If you fail to believe this, try visiting any depressed area after sunset, even during the sunlight, too. It should be remembered that tribal mentality could change one's method of communication and behavior as we cross boundaries.

As Mankin traveled in silence, he remembered the **"butt"** incidence with this lovely older American lady at one of those upbeat discos—a showy scene where every one foolishly pretended to be super cool. Everything was so laid back that many times you could have left these scenes frustrated because you were too cool to make any "connections." Yes, one can be too laid back at times. This lady walked up and asked, "Is it true that my butt is big?"

Mankin remembered smiling and calmly pondering, "Now, what in heaven is a 'butt' in this culture?"

It would be naive to believe she is talking about cigarette butt. She was not even smoking. There were tremendous people at the bars just smiling about this query which was pointedly directed at Mankin. This called for tactfulness, not jumpiness. "Well what do you think?" Mankin remembered saying. "I am asking you!" she responded, earnestly looking into his eyes. The beginning of silence.

At this time everyone started gathering around, forming a semicircle, like a miniature United Nation of all races, creeds, and levels of drunkenness. Mankin's Chinese friend Loon Wauh shouted, "I like these women with big butts; I am a butt man." She looked at him quizzically and turned her head sideways in a mocked smile, saying, "Oh, really?" She meant for him to *butt out,* and leave her alone to get her answer.

As Mankin calmly stared in her eyes, he realized that cultures could really play with one's reality. Words can be transformed to mean so many different things to so many different people. By this time, the friendly Loon was playing the perfect lunatic by encouraging this nonsense quiz by asking, "You have something against this lady's butt?" He was also pandering to the numerous, noisy, ethnocentric American Blacks who were putting their arms on Loon's shoulder, giving high-fives, slapping his palms, or whatever—all saying the same thing in unison, "Brother, what you have against the sister?"

With Loon, the lunatic, playing the popular peon, the beautiful lady put her right hand at her waist, looked sensuously at her rear, and teasingly inquired, "Well what do you think about my butt? Is it big or not?"

Oh, my gosh, so her rear is called her butt! Mankin remembered replying, "Lady, you are beautifully formed. That man has some sense of proportionality, but he lacks the fine descriptive knowledge to tell you what he sees."

She beamed and replied, "Really? You think so?"

Indeed she was beautifully formed. Yes, like being over forty, beautiful and at the top of the sensual game. And knowing it, too! A very delightful but dangerous combination when one thinks that at that level there is generally no fear to let the *game* begin. She claimed her feminine psyche has began its path of true evolvement...

One of the things Mankin remembered about the incident is that this lady was kind enough to help him avoid any great embarrassment by using her body language to hint him that she was referring to her rear. Age has a way of developing great sophistication to minimize friction. Mankin chuckled about this incident and wondered if the brilliant Loon, with all his esoteric computerized knowledge, would have deciphered what a butt is. With the logical Loon, that is almost like a given.

How simple it is to grow up in a culture where all things are laid out for you? Where all the rules are spelled out from the first day and one does not have to sweat bullets or be a quiet observer to avoid being socially offensive to your hosts. Take a common social disparity. To be "fat" in many cultures is related to show affluence and prosperity. Now, we all know that affluence and prosperity is tied to power.

26

So to be fat is possibly a sign of power. Now, here is where everything goes topsy-turvy for the uninformed immigrant who jumped the gun too fast and wanted to be integrated in the imagined melting cauldron of the North American culture. To be considered fat in the North American culture is to be thought of in all of the negative phases one can ever imagine. How about equating fatness to pigs, to indolence, to mental retardation, and even to body odor? It would appear that the only thing positive about fat is being "a fat cat," meaning having a lot of money. And, even the "fat cat" description has a negative connotation. It means that one can be easily convinced to give up one's money without getting equal value in return. Anyone who disbelieves this can look at the numerous businesses that advertise their methods of getting rid of your fat. They will gladly take your money (even what you don't have, in terms of money, may be taken away) but you will still have your fat. Or, perhaps, you may even get fatter! Then you may have to keep tied to these management types who smile and praise your effort to look different from the way you are. In actuality, it's a system to have you hate yourself. You are not being educated about your body; you are being convinced that you are unattractive. The joke is on the dieter, because he or she is paying to be told how odious he or she is. Could it be that these programs are trying to get you mentally and physically fatigued, making it easier to separate you from your cash? Work it!

Mankin remembered being told that all things are manifestation of one's belief system, and one's reality follows what one believes in. This sounds a bit too philosophical and heavy at times but a real-time example may bring home the point more clearly. The scene is Toronto in the College and Spadina area. A recent immigrant called to a pretty Canadian girl just coming from the beauty shop, "Hi, fatty! How you doing?"

"Ahh!" gasped the beautiful one in disbelief. Her blue eyes opened, staring fully focused at her admirer (in this case her tormentor). Her lower jaw dropped for a moment and there were sounds of rushing intake of air to her lungs. She quickly regained her composure and stepped briskly on.

"What did I do? She don't like me, man!" replied the confused immigrant.

He became a bit subdued and would not give eye contact to anyone in his group. He believed he was being rejected as a man. There were a lot of racial theories being bantered about by some of his group. No one bothers to think about the language until a Jamaican lady told him that his approach was incorrect.

She shocked them by saying, "How would you like to be dressed up for a special occasion, and people on the street called you 'ugly' as you passed them? Never call anyone here *fat* unless you mean to curse them."

"But, I didn't mean any harm. I just wanted to tell her how juicy she looked," replied the surprised immigrant.

He was now back to his old self again, because this was the first woman he has ever tried talking with since he migrated. It was comforting to him in knowing he was still in control and can make his moves here the way he once did in his own country.

"Juicy! Mi, Mumma! What a description. What you going to do, eat her?" asked the smiling lady.

"No. I am not a cannibal," retorted the amused migrant.

"I know you are not. I am just joking."

28

"Thank you, Miss B. I must catch her again another time when she passed by," beamed the jubilant immigrant.

"You called me Miss B! What is my name?" asked the lady.

"Well, I don't really know, but you helped me out, man," replied the puzzled immigrant.

"My name is Sharon, but you can call me Shar. You must try to learn the languages and customs of the country you live in, or you won't make it in this life."

"Thanks, Miss B...ah...Sharon," replied the tactless migrant.

"Old habits die hard, I suppose. You take care of yourself," replied Sharon.

The uninformed immigrant was just trying to be nice. He did not give himself enough time to learn the nuances of the two societies he encountered. He was really being kind in his native society, but he ended up being extremely uncouth in the present society. This is a case of jumping the gun and not trying to learn the rules of the game. Perhaps the migrant one had not realized that his native society had prepared him for this sidewalk encounter. Mankin remembered one of his old mentors always talking about "experience teaches wisdom." He also remembered the wily domino pair of "Tumdek" and "Yaga Yaga" who explained that they played the game at the cosmic level. In their **Cosmic Domino** they underrated no opponent, irrespective of how marginal one's playing skill appeared to be. They always calmly watched an opponent before playing, theorizing that their opponent's play might be just a trick in planning an upset. Tumdek and Yaga Yaga always said their opponents were in the contest to either win or lose, but they would not tell Tumdek or Yaga Yaga the truth; therefore, it was the Cosmic Pair's duty to find out. Their last words were, "We know what we are here for!" **A very** definitive statement, saying their intention is to win. Go where winners are!

The migrant one, perhaps, had never played dominoes at home. If he did, he would realize that to play effectively, one should stay on the outside and try to find out who the stalwarts of the game are before jumping in the contest. To do otherwise is to encounter disaster (possibly a non-loving "six-love") or run the risk of being a perpetual loser, because you have chosen the weakest partner and have not studied the playing techniques of your opponents. The end result is your becoming a yo-yo at the table—sitting to play, and then continually being removed after just one set of game. In other words, your play may mirror your life's play—a perpetual loser in every phase. Not a good feeling, is it? Look before you leap. If you do not, then there is always that triumphant voice shouting, "Next loser!" Can anyone guess who that loser is?

As Mankin ponders life's concept on winners, he formed the idea that we create our own universe. He ponders the question of how can an immigrant find happiness in a rootless society where everything keeps changing at a pace that taxes his mental and/or physical capabilities to their limits. He smiles and playfully ponders the idea of living on a commune in California with some of those Zen folks, or whoever, and as some people would jokingly say, "sit and contemplate his navel." That would not be too restful, though, because Mankin had seen a better situation that fits his needs. Zen is great from what Mankin has been told, and commune living has its rewards, also, but living in a commune in North America would be like living in an enclave. Similar to living on the periphery of the main society (a.k.a. an American ghetto). People from less industrialized countries know about serenity of life. Their's are idyllic surroundings that do not match their ideal situation. They travel for economic improvement as advertised in the glossy pages of magazines and find nightmarish side effects that they could not have imagined. They find ghettoes that are ferociously guarded by the robotics institutional functionaries under the titles of social workers and police organizations. As the puppet immigrants march to these puppeteers, Mankin wonders if this type of life pleases the conscience of these travelers, or are they too afraid to return to their native land? Mankin already knows some of the answers to these questions. We all know that everything cannot be obtained in one place, but how long are you going to suffer depravity, injustice, and destruction of your young in reaching for the vanishing point of economic viability coupled with self-esteem? This position is very difficult to obtain, and maintain, in industrialized countries. Could it be that we are being trained to view our self-worth as an indication of our bank accounts. If this is so, then it has not made most immigrants happy, because they do not have the numbers in the banks to make it enhance their self-worth. So why are they staying on then? Perhaps they still remember their earlier life and know it is still better where they are now.

Perhaps we all need to try doing things differently when we start believing we have tried everything and nothing worked. The questions are: Is this what you really wanted? Is this what you think it is? Were you worse off in your old country? The last question is not meant to ask "are you better off." It really means "worse off," because at this stage you have more toys, which you cannot enjoy, because the financial ghouls are always dunning you for your last piece of silver. If one month you are late with your "silver," they will send you asinine notes with insipid hints of friendliness, possibly scaring the daylights out of you. Yes, putting your spirit in a realm of darkness called "bad credit risks." This is where the numbering systems put lifelong demerit marks against your efforts to live comfortably in this strange society. Even when you pay them, the avaricious scoundrels will not leave you alone. They send telegram-looking letters to your door, asking you to spend more money with them. Now, we all know what telegrams meant to older immigrants. This type of letter, again, scares the life out of you, because you now believe that your old parents have died, and you have to make preparation to bury them. Now, you really have to buy something from the scoundrels—high potency vitamins to help your stressed-out body. Yes, and while you are there, the commercial maniac may want you to buy some acidophilus and bifidus to remove the side effects of the vitamins from your nervous body. Dance. The puppeteer is pulling your string. You did not hear the music, you said? The music is not for you to hear puppet; your movement is for the puppeteer to enjoy. You volunteered for this remembered by saving your scarce dollars or pounds to travel to 'paradise' overseas. Do you remember the look of envy on your friends' faces as you left home to dance to the puppeteer's music? How long ago was that?

Mankin recalled the time when one of his lady acquaintances were having problems adjusting to the overseas culture shock where people can be extremely polite but ever so cold and calculating. She mentioned to her friend that she was having some distressing problems due to pregnancy. She also had no health insurance, no immigration papers, and no established place to live. And, of course, with little or no money, here, no one was willing to help. She was stressed out to the max. She exclaimed between tears, "I have tried everything and nothing seems to work."

"Have you tried prayer?" her friend asked.

"Well, no," replied the frustrated lady.

"When everything else fails, always try the simplest thing," replied the friend.

Mankin smiled, reminding himself that prayer is really a radical response to the Creator. Pray on!

"That is the only thing left to try."

"That is not true!" shouted her friend.

"What?" asked the weepy-eyed pregnant one.

"We were always friends, and you did not asked me for help. I have a place to live, and we are all women, so I understand, too."

"You mean you will... I didn't want to ask, because people change over here."

"Yes, we all change. Even you, too. You are now pregnant, that, too, is a change. Would you help me if I was in your position?"

"Yes!"

"Really? So why do you think I would not help you?"

"Well..."

"Agree. You will be well! Just remember friendship," laughed the helpful friend.

Communication and cooperation are sadly lacking among the migrant groups, especially when some feel they have been here long enough to "dismiss" their old friends and migrate to a different social level. Many migrants forget they reached Overseas because of the old weekly "pardner" system. Now, that was cooperation to the max. Mankin would agree that, now, there is new business awareness, so the old system might not be as effective here as in the old country. Unfortunately, for many migrants, the new, trendy business awareness comes with complicated business costs and high taxation. The business "suits" that administer these businesses are cash-cold money-mechanics who have no feeling for your neighborhood—that means you, your family, and friends. On the other hand, it seems that the level of honesty and cooperation displayed in our quaint little Overseas villages were never transported to our adopted homes. One friend told another that he was not afraid to trust him; he was afraid to trust his new family condition where his grown children are always getting into trouble and had to be bailed out of jail. He did not want to lose him as a friend after 40 years, so to avoid that, he would not again allow him to be his "pardner" banker. It seems the friend and his wife, many times, had to "borrow" funds to bail out their errant children. The parents' honesty was intact but the temptation to always *borrow* to help their troubled children caused serious problems with their friends. In the villages this was never a problem, their family was never under that social or criminal pressure. As the migrant circle became more diverse, there was an unwillingness to trust each other, but some cooperation is still in style. The simplest way out of many problems is through cooperation. It was very pleasing to see how these two friends came together to compare notes and find a common solution to a problem that had caused so many immigrant women headaches. Their solution was spiritual, humane, and righteous. The only thing that was confounding was imagining that a problem existed when there was none. Sometimes we suffer because we have not exercised our options. We choose to live in the past and never bother to look objectively at the changes that took place in our homeland while we were away. Why stay in any one place and suffer when we really have other options to be tried.

As Mankin contemplated this decision, he heard Simnally park his car in the driveway. Simnally was dressed in a pair of brown boots and carried a military cap under his arm. Mankin could only smile as he reflected on how rebellious Simnally had been in his youth. Simnally with a military cap under his arm? Is this a militant stance against the military industrial complex, or what? This is the same Simnally who the British military tried to conscript in England; the Simnally who evaded them for...well, for the whole life of the draft.

"Wait, the one Kenworth fade out from us this day?" Simnally ask while looking through the window.

"Simnally, you want some fish?" shouted a feminine voice from the kitchen.

"How come you never tell me that your relative is here?" Simnally asked Mankin. "How you doing, Reane, you sweet thing?" said Simnally as he accepted a plate of fried fish and a bottle of Guinness.

Mankin knew that Reane was the first woman that ever cooked for Simnally since he left England to reside in Canada. Theirs was a bond of friendship that was deeper than sexual gratification. They had already decided that as two married people in a strange country with mates overseas they did not wish that type of entanglement, especially as both mates would be coming soon. But, of course, that did not stop Simnally from sweet-talking Reane.

"Gal, I tell you, if you were ten years older, and I was twenty years older, you would not get away from me so easily."

"Who talking, now? You or the Guinness?" asked Reane.

"Look, the rose in June is not so sweet as..."

"What we have here, now? The recalcitrant Simnally turning into a kitchen poet over a plate of fish and a bottle of British tarry brew," chided a laughing Kenworth, poking his head through the kitchen doorway.

"You missed the point, you Master race lover. I am here talking to a beautiful woman of my race. A man has to show respect to earn respect and respect is due this lady," remarked Simnally through a mouthful of fried fish."

"Tell me anything you Black imperialist! I see your white Masters taught you some of their euphemistic tricks. The only problem is that you are using it on your own people in a trivial sense to get food from your friends," laughed Kenworth while looking into his friend's plate.

"You want some of this fish. It's the last?" Simnally asked Kenworth as he proffered the plate.

"Oh man, thank you, Simnally."

"You rapacious scoundrel! Now, you claimed I deceived the race to get food, but you are willing to accept the same food from me. I think one of the tenets of the Malcolm X doctrine was self-sufficiency," shouted Simnally in triumph.

"Talk to him, yes, Simnally. Ken there is a lot of fish over there. Want some?" asked a smiling Reane.

"Thanks"

"Simnally, you are devious. No, make that deadly. You use too much sophistry to bring out your point," chided Kenworth.

"You want something to drink, Kenworth. We have carrot juice with white rum," said Reane.

"Now, you talking girl."

"What happened? The Master race can't give you fish and white rum, Ken?" asked Simnally.

"I tell you before that you like to stratify people in groups too much. Renew your thinking, man. While you were asleep in Britain things have changed, and your mind is still in the *backra* days."

"Yes, things have changed for the worse. That is why I am reminding you to be aware, and don't get taken in by the media. They overload you with all this rubbish, and you misinterpreted it for information that will enhance your quality of life. Kenworth, whenever you come out of the Rip van Winkel-state, we can talk intelligently."

Reane started playing the song, "Rivers of Babylon." As Mankin listened to the music, his thoughts flew to a more relaxed and happier time. He shook his head, as he now concluded that he was really happy then. The problem was he did not know it. His mentor was right when he said, "Experience teaches wisdom." The music was low and soothing. Looking at the album cover he observed that the flutist was a white person. The Skatalite group he knew was a giant in the Ska and reggae music field. He sincerely wished they were well paid for this music, because the fusion with the flute was truly outstanding. He looked at the hairstyles of the players and drifted off to earlier days when great players played songs like "Eastern Standard Time," "Scrap Iron," and many more good tunes with the dominant trombone player, Don Drummond. As he poured some of his drinks out the window to remember those that had gone before, he smiled and focused his mind to the group of Rastas on the hill in his neighborhood. He could plainly see them and hear their voices, now, as they shook their locks in defiance at the British "Babylonian" System, while beating their rhythmic drums in unison entreating, "Come over if you are sober, and take a draw of this here 'Cali-over'!"

Then came the untiring responsive chants of "Hear ye, Ma" as the pulsating drums answered each other throughout the darkness of the night. The brethren resonated in the **Nyabinghi** ways of purifying themselves and calling on the great Forces of the Most High, Jah, to power down the "**downpressors**" the way HE did in the past to the Colonialist Suffocators of East Africa. Of course, they were smoking the ganja plant, but none of these guys were the criminal, dope-dealing-types who are generally associated with the North American urban ghettoes. Mankin remembered the police organization raiding the Rasta's camp, causing some people in the neighborhood to be very upset. They complained so bitterly that the authorities were truly embarrassed. One knows how it goes; politicians have to be elected, so they do not push the common people too far during election time. The next day, the Rastas were all released to the contrived political chants of how the "voice of freedom triumphs" and "how the System works." It certainly does work, especially when politicians are running neck-and-neck to the wire during election time! Anyway, that night, the uncompromising "Beards" attracted numerous new converts while celebrating their victory over the Babylonian miscreants. Mankin remembered this incident as the first encounter with the dichotomy of life. People really wanted the Rastas to go away, but they actually wanted no interference from the authorities in moving them. On the other hand, others in the neighborhood wanted the Rastas to stay because their relatives were in the group.

That night, the group did a special rendition of the "Lion of Judah" with free, carrot-size "spliff" for everyone. Guess who showed up? The political groups trying to take credit for releasing the drummers. Some of the "Beards" openly denounced the politicians as creepy "back and belly rats!" Those days were long ago when people were very idealistic—long before Mankin realized that politics is fakery by talking friendly to everyone to perpetuate a given system without actually changing anything. It is a kind of old-boy system (There is not many old-girl power system around at this time.) of compromises to maintain the power brokers. Perhaps a certain "Beard" was right when he referred to politics, as mere "poly-tricks." It seems like common sense to believe that when dealing with trickery, honesty definitely will have to awaits it's turn.

Mankin realized that sometimes one has to question reality when euphemism reigns and honesty takes a backseat. This is nothing new to humanity, so life must continue, but one has to remember one's limitation. In trying to maximize large bank accounts, the migrants mortgage their children's future to an oppressive and often futile existence by staying long in stressful situations, and hoping for a Utopian ending, which generally only happens in the movies, and most times only for a specific hue. The other hue generally dies off early in the show, for Hollywood determines the show was not about him anyway. Happiness is a myth if you are a ghetto dweller, as most immigrants are. How long should anyone live in any country before they can migrate to better neighborhoods, especially if one works assiduously for this goal? It seems that migrants are not evaluated by their intellects, but by their color, their country of origin, and their culture. Unfortunately most migrants do help in stratifying themselves by following the examples set up by their former colonial masters. Moron sees, moron does!

Living in the ghetto is living in the metropolis with mega-trauma where the migrants form a liaison with the core of the spiritless system, which finally destroys the last vestige of their self-awareness. The migrants then become compulsively neurotic about superficial commercial trinkets, which is supposed to give a sense of achievement. This sense of false security and of achievement is propagated throughout the family structure to the detriment of their young who are fed this rubbish of actually believing that everything is all right as long as you and your groups can own the latest fashion. This cycle of excess buying, perhaps, is an attempt to soothe their spiritual and social disconnection from the homeland. The unfortunate side effect of these silly behaviors is crime. The children are so caught up with the 'in style' bequeathed to them by their parents that they would risk going to prison than to be out of style. The children do not view honesty in the same way as their parents from the old country did. Prison to them is a badge of honor.

Mankin remembered the utterance of an old immigrant in Hartford, Connecticut, who sadly shook his head muttering, "The ghetto styles of my fellow compatriots are just a veneer—an abstraction of the past—to cover the social and spiritual disconnection of a lost generation who continue to dream of acceptance in a strange and hostile land where everything is quantified but never qualified for a better mental state." Very much so it seems. Business acumen rules and the human spirit becomes stunted on the altar of "the person with the most toys wins!"

The inculcation of the young with this type of drivel resulted in an absolute rejection of their parents' culture, where honesty, respect for elders, self-respect, and a general respect for all life forms are paramount to living. Most of the children have book knowledge (if they attended school) but are spiritually empty. Now, the parents are all wondering how the children are so different from themselves, like aliens from far-away stars.

Migration is good for many countries with their burgeoning population and abject poverty. On the other hand, it wrecks many families who migrated. The migrant, many times, has small, socially well adjusted children who have to be left initially behind with grandparents, family members, or friends for the first few years during migration.

Now, here is the problem; generally, no one can take care of young ones as well as the parents. Most times, after the parents' migration, the children feel insecure and start misbehaving. By the time you get them Overseas, they are little hooligans ready for destruction in the ghetto where you reside. Now, the dilemma is what to do with them here? You dare not discipline them! If you do, you will not see them again. The system will put you away; far away, and then finally remove them from you. That may not be too bad, but don't rejoice yet! Just be careful here. The System may get nasty by charging you a steep 'storage fee' for them, and then finally 'warehouse' you for being too excessive. Note that being 'excessive' here means you did too little or too much to the young ones...too much attention or too little attention, whatever. (*What happens if you do just enough? Now, that is where the problem is!*) Anyway, during this warehousing period, their media friends will be telling the universe that you are some type of 'young human molester!' Or, the children may just decide to run away...now, there is an option. Still not too good...the system hates paperwork! They like physical stats. Dead or alive, just show them a body. Now, don't get curious and try to deal with any dead bodies here; this is where the Z-dimension occurs. If you ever show the System a young dead body you are in the zero dimension. Final game for you! Mankin has to give the System credit for its protection of children. The System gets an 'A' here. Drum rolls! Most migrants have no new idea about disciplining their children. They practiced too much of the 'Kunta Kinte' way. If you are one of those forceful slave-beating Kunta Kinte-way types, be warned not to use the multiple personality defense that your *'other'* personality did it. If you should get away with this one from the judge, the powerful Tax Collecting people will be sending your 'other' personality a bill. They will want to know why he or she has evaded paying taxes all these years. Back to the judges again…just your luck it may be the same judge.

Now, what have you really gained from migration so far? The sights?

Mankin heard this conversation in Ottawa between two expatriates from two different countries who lamented how their young ones are not really people they could trust.

"How are your children doing, now?" asked the first lady.

"I do not have children; I have strangers at my gates," replied lady number two.

"How come? What's wrong?"

"They are all heartless, North American people. They have no respect or love except for money, mi dear. I really believe the doctors and nurses swapped my children at the hospital. My husband claimed that I had children for another man, because he saw none of his people with these types of attitude," the second lady lamented with watery eyes.

"Sometimes I wonder about the swap, too, myself. No help, no love, no favor except for money. You ever wonder if we actually wasted our time having them? I never thought about abortion as a young woman, but now, when I look at them, I really do. God, forgive me!" said the first lady as her voice trailed off in a whisper while she wiped her eyes with the back of her hand, and her friend moved in closer to comfort her by putting an arm across her shoulder.

"Love conquers all, hon. Love makes it easy. Don't cry; it will make them feel powerful."

"You right. Time is the master factor. Time will soon catch up to them, too. Their own children may come and do the same to them, although am not praying for that. But, if it happens, it happens," agreed the first lady, in a more upbeat manner.

"Well, mi not saying mi not praying for that. You right; if it happens, then it happens. God has ways of dealing with wicked people. Ha! Ha! Mi nuh want anything to happen to them, though. But, they must feel it; they are too horrible," shouted a smiling second lady.

"I wonder how did I get these people?"

"What! You did not try sex? Ha! Ha! Don't tell mi you forgot those summers in Toronto," interrupted the first lady with great laughter.

"Hmm, fire!" shouted the first lady, waving her hands over her head and laughing with great gusto.

"We must meet always and talk as we did many years ago. It is nice seeing you again. Don't ever get lost again, please. We are the real people over here. Children are just too busy to be concerned about us anymore. Here is my address and phone number."

"My dear, we have been through too much to be separated at this stage of the game. Here is my number and address, also. I just live around the corner from here. We can even walk over there now. Come on let mi show you where."

The first lady held her friend's hand and joyfully walked away to show her home.

Mankin wondered if these ladies spoiled their children with all the latest toys during their formative years, and turned them into present-day monsters that are devoid of all feelings for their parents and humanity in general. How many times must we listen to a mother's excuses, always coming up with some new version of a fairy tale excusing themselves and their children for their aberrant and criminal behaviors—blaming others or falling back on yesterday's silly excuses that "someone puts them so!" How they waste their small savings, or borrowing large sums of money, on useless 'readings' from some 'reader woman' who is supposed to be able to influence the outcome of a legal trial that is perhaps already heavily stacked against their child. It is time to be concerned and wonder if the future of the parents of these 'robotics ones' resides in the hard, cold 'old people concentration camps' called convalescent homes; where they warehouse old tax payers who can no longer effectively produce. Once they get you into these camps (many times against your will) the young ones use the System of unscrupulous lawyers to legally disinherit you and possibly unceremoniously prepare you for some frozen plot of land, or an efficient oven to cremate your remains, while they ghoulishly divvy up your belongings with plans for the latest cars and/or apartments without actually paying respect to the departed soul. Again, the Cyborg with the most toys wins! The puzzling question is—how can a people change so much over just one generation or less? It would appear that the only connection between parents and children is the name. Too many immigrants have strangers within their gates. They have the same names, but they are strangers, because family cooperates for the betterment of the group. Too many immigrants are just busy with only mundane activities. They lack the insight to get back to basics and find themselves. There are things that your little pittance of pay will not buy you or your young ones. Working yourself to death to pay only bills will get you an early cremation and hastened your burial in an unceremonious plot with strangers to mourn your passing.

Mankin long ago realized that a person has to know his or her limitations. He vividly remembered his Indian friend

Patel saying: "Sometimes we need to listen to our heart song, not just its rhythmic sounds, but the inner voice. Don't let your heart song be drowned out by the stress traffic to satisfy the ego. A man must know himself and must be aware of his dharma."

Yes, Patel was right; a person must be aware of his life's path. Over the years, Mankin found that it is true, we all should do the things that give us lasting happiness and bring us closer to the highest truth. We, as immigrants, cannot continue to live as if we are happy in a land where we are always running with the thunderous herd. After years, we need a rest to graze in a quiet pasture once again so that we can hear our heart song. Remove the ego from the systematic business competition and move back to reality, because your tomorrow is now. Remove the programmed filter that encourages you to rejoice in silly commercial slogans like "shop till you drop" —so superficial and childish, but very expensive.

Can you remember the last time you tried to mimic a bird's song, and rejoiced in your heart's song? Have you really laughed recently? Not the cultivated and studied facial contortion to show costly dental work, but real laughter, until tears ran down your cheeks. A real "kiss mi laughter!" Mankin realized that most immigrants do not laugh anymore; they are too busy trying to cope with little details of life which culminated into big issues for them. One wonders if some of them are ever emotionally moved by anything. Or, are they just coexisting as jaded wage slaves whose prime directive is toil to pay the bills in some low-rent, crime-ridden urban area plagued by gunfire, dope dealers, and the incessant presence of the institutional murderers? Most immigrants are not from the ghettoes in their own countries, so one has to wonder how do they acclimatized to such a condition. They must have longed to move to the suburbs with trees and quietness to their thoughts. They must have wanted to live in a place where they could listen to their heart's song. With this type of stress, it is no wonder that many immigrants are flocking to stress management classes.

Perhaps they need to be told that stress management is only needed after mismanagement of one's life. Mankin sees the answer as removing one's self to another location, preferably the original point, to home—wherever that is. As one gets older, the urban areas become even more dangerous! As Ras Zeig usually said in the days gone by, "Grab a skirt and leave earth, because macah dah yah!" Yes, leave with your love one, because it is difficult here at this time in our lives to continue living (or existing) in a cocoon when there is happiness out there. As he nostalgically drifted to those early days, he mentally pictured his home, not as the present tourist Mecca as advertised, but as a habitable place of residence where fun was the order of the day. Yes, we all grow up during our lifetime so things will change, or we will change, too, but something is amiss when it appears that, internationally, our only positive portrayal is a land for certain type of music and as a tourist resort. Is that all we have to offer?

IMAGERY:

Has anyone ever wondered why the beauty queens of these islands are not of the general complexion of the masses? Neither do they have curly or short hair. The commercial boys fancy the European look, and the people of African descent seem to agree that "Black is not universally acceptable as being beautiful." Is racism rampant here, also? It seems the Europeans won again, or possibly the Europeans *are* more attractive! Anyway which group sets up this pageant? He who organizes the pageant may wish to "organize" the winner too. Mankin knows this is not a heavyweight championship-boxing match. But organizers rule!

The class and racial groups with the darker skin are always at the bottom rung. Is there a universal message here? The immigrants' little, ingrained, unproductive games of color, where they are still looking for the curly hair (which women generally refer to as "good hair") straight nose-type, are still in vogue. Old habits are hard to break. Now, you know why so many of them swear by their hot comb and chemicals—their transformation tools for migrating to the power group. Immigrants are always acting as amnesiacs by forgetting things, which hurt them throughout their course of history. As someone once said, they still have "the little housemaid/slave mentality of wanting the approval of the European patriarch." We know the utilitarian excuse, too— "my hair is unruly (not *knotty*, that would be equating it with a negative) so processing it makes it more manageable." How about, "You shouldn't complain, because that is what men want! We did it for you." Really, now? Isn't it time you do something for yourself? This topic caused Mankin to chuckle, and he place-shifted away from an impending gender skirmish.

Gender skirmish is generally fake public verbiage resulting in both genders privately coming together in obeying the primal command to settle their differences. Body response wins. "You cuss mi in public, and now, look how you a behave with me in private!" Come on.

The islands are portrayed, as places of paradise for the ruling race, where the simple, smiling people of the dominated working race are always willing to work for peanuts to comfort the dominant race. How come the working group (or nationals) is never shown having the nice time? Perhaps their enjoyment is serving the rulers. The images shown to people are very important. The young have the great desire to always copy the behaviors shown on television or in other media hypes. One just has to look and see some of the destructive behaviors, exhibited by the entertainment industries, which are quickly adopted by young people to reinforce their already dysfunctional behaviors. If imagery contributed to deviant behaviors, then how come all of these islands are always showing their nationals as servants in some minimal role while the other race is always having all the fun? Many people of the servant-class race are also tourists, but they are generally never given places of prominence in any of the tourists' brochures! This is a sore point with many nationals whenever they talk about their countries. Imagine your own country acting as if it is only the dominant race that existed. This lack of respect for their own people seems to permeate all the tourist island nations in the Caribbean Basin. It is understood that all tourist countries will have their people working in that industry. So we may speculate it could be difficult to differentiate guests from visitors in homogeneous society, but these islands are not. It is important in your tourist brochures to show other races being entertained, too. They paid, too, didn't they! One has to really think about the public relations agency that generated these brochures. What race are they, and whom do they take their directions from? The main question here is who makes decisions for the interests of the people in these islands? Is anyone home! The old adage "money talks, and others obey" is alive and doing well in this situation.

Mankin sat by the large trees and watched the birds fly with swift wings from tree to tree and branches to branches in search of food. They whistled and flew in tandem as the mating urge magnified itself in the early springtime. He wondered, as he watched them perched high up in the branches, if they have names to call each other. The wind made whistling sounds between the leaves and branches while disturbing them to form complex geometric shapes to confuse the mind.

Mankin wondered aloud about the boundaries of reality and virtuality as he watched sunrays dance and glisten off the moving branches, forming blinding, reflecting spots, which shut out any recognition of the wonders of light and shadows. He knew the activities he witnessed here are real. Many things these days are so much virtual reality, or if you dare to think about it—inactive activity, which peak your interest, but you can take no physical part in the action. Have you ever thought about how you watch the cinema or your "one-eyed monster" —the television? You take no part in the action, but it certainly takes a great deal of your time. It can control a human being. As the bald-pate bird glanced at him from a safe distance, from the highest rung of branches in the tallest tree, Mankin recalled a beach scene that always seem to fight his subconscious for equal time in the real world. He remembered a gull flying gracefully across the beach and an immigrant Ras I Zabalu looking skyward and saying, "Ride the wings of destiny to alight on a shore of peace."

He was actually referring to his status as an immigrant, leaving his home to find peace, prosperity and happiness overseas. He actually was externalizing his wish list, which he hoped the gull would find better luck in fulfilling than he did. He was equating flight with easy transition.

At this time, everyone looked up into to the sky until some one sighed and said: "The community sees us not as soaring eagles, but as starlings. Not as darling starlings either."

Mankin ponder the comparison of eagles and starlings. He knew the starlings here are small black birds that are very low on the food chain, whereas the eagles here are large majestic birds, which are high on the food chain with high political visibility. There are no black eagles here.

"Perhaps we are our worst enemy," continued I Zabalu, looking skyward at a pair of birds flying in a tight formation.

"What! How come you're saying that when most of us fight so hard to get here, only to find, the longer we stay here, that we can never be happy?" asked an irate Belizean.

Mankin smiled and remarked to himself, "Been too long at the fair my dear." We all became starlings as the time progressed. The only reward is we recognized the transmigration from eagles to starlings, and most of us had made plans to recapture our former position.

"We often failed to cooperate as a group. We became suspicious, simplistic, and materialistic. Worst, we lost our love for others, as the dollar flows. We did not give our children the good values we inherited from our parents. We went too plastic, trying to adopt a new value system. Look at those two birds flying together. Cooperation, sister, cooperation will get you there," intoned the Zabalu as he pointed skyward at the flying birds. Someone lamented, "Whose fault is it if they don't want those values?" That is a valid question!

Mankin had heard these parental discussions so many times. How many young ones in the immigrant community had laughed scornfully, saying: "Damn those 'old country values.'" One serious-minded mother once reiterated, "...then don't call me from your demeaning prison cells crying and asking for help. If 'fancy pants' takes you out of your game, then deal with it as the adult you claim you are...and by the way, stop blaming the System, because the majority of the time you were guilty.

Parents are no fools; we know the truth many times, but we always wish otherwise. Understand! You believe we are simpletons because we are always helping you. You ridicule us, because we never went to school here. If you are so smart, Mr. Foreign-born, how come you are being treated as a slave and don't even know it? How come you and your friends are always going to prison, while we 'old foolish' Island-born ones are free to go and come, as we like? You are cruel, weak, and useless!"

Yes, pure common sense and hard facts help to take away the excuse for a budding criminal career.

"Ras I, you have a good point, man. Things are not lovely here at all, but we have to live," said the Belizean with finality.

"Live! My sister is not happy here, although she made all that money," mentioned the sister of the Belizean, as she kicked up sands with her well-manicured toe.

"They did not promise you happiness; they promised you more dollars. Your happiness is your business. We are the community that we love to blame. Everyone seems to think when one comes here that more dollars is going to give them more happiness. I thought so too."

The l Zabalu sees the picture in the correct frame of mind. The immigrants, for too many times, tend to blame others for their misfortunes and fail to take a hard look at their choice of options. We cannot have it all, which is everything in one place at all times. The community may have reason to ostracize a certain group because of deviant behaviors to their norms. After all, we are sometimes the interlopers in their country. We left our country with the desire to make it at all costs. We often failed to make the transition to a happier life, because we equated happiness only with economics, and did not do our homework in viewing the overall consequences of competition in a strange land. The strange and diverse society took its toll on our energy and taxed our meager resources to their limits. We became just statistics, as we left our broken dreams and bodies as relics on the sands of time like monuments to the unfulfillment of broken dreams and promises. We pioneered passes for others to follow, and hopefully they will have succeeded where we failed, by avoiding the pitfalls where we faltered...but at this time they seem to have found a new way to bury themselves with dope!

"The problem with us is that we all felt cut off from home. Our loved ones could not be easily reached. We are incomplete and always lonely. 'Country is fine for what it offers us,'" stated the nattily dressed Bermudan as he brushed sand from his neatly pressed jeans.

Mankin looked across the group to see his Trinidadian friend Ramnarine removing his dark glasses, wiping his eyes, smiling, and then beginning to explain in a quiet voice: "We lost our bearings when we only chased the dollars. We moved between sky and earth in a random pattern to the beat of an economic drum. We have no reasoning anymore. We only react to the jingles of coins and the things we can buy. Boy, we lost our spirit and focus. Time to stop beating ourselves, start thinking, and give thanks that we finally see the light."

"We have to minimize the greed factor, and enhance the spirit, man," suggested Ras Zabalu.

Mankin looked up the beach and saw a lady trying to ride an unwilling horse, which decided to go home rather than obey the rider. He considered this scenario and wondered if we are all unwilling horses for the leisurely class. Perhaps we should also go home to consolidate our happiness. But for us, who have been so long at "the fair," the question still remains, "where is our home?" For many of us, our mortgaged houses are not homes. They are the System's economic traps to drain our energy and confuse our spirits for 30 years. One whole generation in time…but certainly a life-force in energy.

Many immigrants had the view portrayed in those glossy magazines, and other forms of propaganda, which painted the industrial world as Utopia. They were deceived. Anyway, they still have a choice to leave if they are unhappy. Unfortunately this is easier said than done, especially for those who severed all ties with their place of birth, both psychologically and physically. There are those immigrants who erase every connection from their homeland—racial heritage, nationality, old friendship, and even family members. As they grow older, there seems to be a strong psychic pull, as if one's soul is calling out for reconnection…the seeking of a spiritual bond of calmness and quietness before traveling towards the final phase.

Marcus Garvey was right in his assumption that all Black people were not suited for returning "home." Where is home? An individual has to define his inner-self, where he wants to be, and which heartbeat or music (drums) he wants to march to. To avoid the trap of sorrows, decide wisely while your energy is still at its peak.

Mankin can still remember the story told him by his grandmother, warning him to always be cautious about joining any gathering without questioning why people are gathering. She told the story of how the British came to her Village Square playing drums and fifes. All the young men ran towards the Square to see the event. The British soldiers encircled them and forcibly enlisted them in the army. Always question the motives before you desire to join any group. Look who is playing the music (beating the drums) before you run to dance. Yes, look before you leap! Listen to the beat from afar before running to the beat, or you may end up being beaten by those who organize the "beat."

While Mankin pondered life's transitional phases, a loud whirring, mechanized sound caused the whole group to focus their vision on a pair of shiny-black attired "wave runners," steering their machines toward a feeding cormorant. The startled bird erratically struggled in an uncoordinated way to quickly gain altitude and get out of the way of the noisy mechanized monster whose rider's only objective was pleasure. How utterly childish and cruel to think only of pleasure while running carelessly over another living being with your latest acquired, mechanized toy. This is the same type of mentality that allows animals to be tortured for sports (hunting) and for profits (experimentation.) As the old frog saying goes, "What is joke to people is death to the frog."

As the noisy machines destroyed the tranquility of the beach, someone remarked, "The machine changed our world, and our spirit followed."

"Like a marriage—for better or worse! Our spirit and the machines will have to co-exists as we follow our destiny," whispered Mankin's inner voice. We can no longer play the part of the shortsighted Luddites.

With his nostalgic thoughts still playing in his mind, Mankin decided to pay another visit to the land of his birth. The travelers queued up to board the midnight flight to the busy tourist areas. As the economy class passengers moved through First Class they all commented on the stand-offish attitude of a man in First Class. This well-suited passenger was acting as if he thought someone was going to borrow his suit. No, friend, it is too hot in the tropics for a suit this time of the year anyway—shades of old British Colonialism. This man was so nervous that his eyes rovingly scanned the group of moving passengers, as if expecting danger. Mankin overheard a fellow passenger whisper that the suited wonder was some despised bureaucrat ("ginigog") who worked for the IMF. "...One of those wicked ginigogs from Overseas, who helped assassinate poorer countries..."

"So, why is he so afraid? Is he afraid of flying?"
"No, he is afraid of us, the people."
"Why? Nobody is doing anything to him?"
"Nobody is trying to hurt him, but the evil fleeth where none pursueth."

The conversation ended when a blue-eyed British youth shook his head, deriding the IMF man by saying, "King Pharaoh, power down and drop your crown!" The two

"Whisperers" made eye contact with the young blue-eyed one, then smiled in recognition of another brother.

There was an air of relaxation as every one gets into light, hearted discussion about their last trip or what they expect this trip to be like. The brochures they read seem to enrapture them about relaxing under trees, riding donkeys, laying on the white sand beaches, surfing, or even smoking some of the illicit smokes. A young woman voiced her concerns about the hazard of traveling through the forest from Montego Bay to her hotel in Ocho Rios. She had never been on the trip before, but had heard how perilous the trip can be. She was not afraid to make the trip. She and her group were just psyching up themselves to overcome the challenging road ahead. When someone mentioned that there were no forests or jungles to overcome, she was a bit deflated, drew out her map to show the area along the sea coast where the sea surrounded the forest, or jungle as she puts it. Many seasoned travelers in various levels of inebriation, and ranges of color changes, joined the conversation to reflect on the topography of the area of concern by their young fellow traveler. One seasoned, older couple, seeing the disappointment on the young lady's face when everyone was trying to convince her there were no jungles or forests to overcome here, started talking about their days of peril in Kenya. They, then, tactfully talked about the similarity of the landscape to her present situation. The young one and her group shouted with glee and started preparing themselves, mentally and physically, for the battle against nature by flexing their muscles and taking deep controlled breathing exercises for the climb on some imaginary **Kilimanjaro.** One of the timid ones of her group inquired about the types of animal in the area. By this time the older couple had relinquished the conversation to the younger, noisy folks. Mankin quietly shook his head in appreciation of "gray power." Give all rightful respect and wisdom to the aged. Some wise acre in the group shouted, "Ride mi donkey!"

The timid one replied smiling, "Oh my. You do not mean a little burro?"

A cool Californian in the group calmly stated, "I will ride nothing that has a brain."

"If the horse don't pull, you have to carry your load," replied his friend in a singing note.

Mankin observed the scene in a quiet and thoughtful manner. He wondered about the people who sell dream trips that sometimes turn into nightmares for the travelers. What will this young woman find to soothe her expectations for the environment that she so desires? Will she supplant it with something else of equal interest? While pondering these ideas, the metallic voice of the stewardess punctured the eerie stillness of the dimly lit cabin, over the steady drone of the engines, with the instruction, "The captain has turned on the no smoking sign, blah, blah..."

Mankin wondered how humanity could put a man on the moon but could not design a decent audio system where one can hear clear instructions in a plane, in an airport, or even in a stadium. Immediately he recalled that in all three places the addressees are a captive audiences. In actuality, the audiences are waiting for something to happen. They are not masters of their own destinies.

There were shuffling activities as everyone settled into their harnesses to comply with the pre-landing regulations. A euphoric feeling grabbed the whole cabin as passengers started looking through the windows and chatting gleefully with each other. The plane flew so low before landing that fishes in clear blue Caribbean Sea could be clearly seen from the portholes. After a slightly bumpy landing, the doors opened to inundate the passengers with fresh tepid tropical air, while passengers jockeyed to get off as quickly as possible. Ever wonder why people are always trying to rush out of planes, trains, or buses? Especially planes. We cannot fly, and we have defied the naturalness of gravity and won. We have been lucky to escape so far, so let's not push our luck. Let's get out of this enclosed box (coffin!) as quickly as we can. Just a thought.

One of the African-American passengers exclaimed, "Oh my Lord! So, it is true. There are countries with a sea of Black people."

As she started humming one of those Negro spirituals, Mankin felt a deep spiritual empathy towards her. Here is a lady who had never left her country, and therefore, never got the experience living in a country where her racial group is in the majority. This is not necessarily a positive, but it definitely can be!

Her traveling companion, who had been quiet throughout the trip, eventually made the statement, "Grandma, here no one will ever refer to us as African-Americans. Everyone will call us by our given names. We will never be classified along racial lines, either. We will be known by our deeds."

The older lady kept on humming her song, kissed her granddaughter on the forehead, looked her steadfastly in the eyes, and smilingly replied, "We would be known by our misdeeds also."

Mankin realized there a private message there between family members. A somewhat mild reprimand for past misdeed or possibly a warning that there are rules here, also, so please do not get careless or disrespectful while we are here. As this quiet matriarch foot touched the tarmac, she dropped a political bombshell by saying,"Child do you know that Marcus Garvey was born here. Yes, on this island!"

"Yes mom, I know that."

"But do you know who he was, and what he represented?"

"Certainly, Grandma. He was the forerunner to MLK."

"Very good child. I am a bit surprised, especially when you put it in a type of biblical context. What else do you know about him, Sisine?"

"He was Black…"

A freckled white youth calmly said, "…even the Rastafarian Movement was an off-shoot of Garvey's UNIA movement in the early 30s. Tell her that."

Everyone including the busy passengers looked with surprise at the freckled Caucasian youth. Possibly thinking how did he get into this radical, super Black politics? The attentive matriarch showed her appreciation of the young Freckled One by bowing her head to him in respect of his knowledge. A pensive bearded passenger kept shaking his head with appreciation saying, "Profound respect, man, profound respect."

The quiet Freckled One was mildly embarrassed, as he shyly looked around at the smiling passengers.

Mankin is quite aware that most African heritage persons are unaware that the European groups know Afro-history. This is a critical Afro-group error because the Euro-groups are the ones who generally determine and write Afro-history. In other words they influence it, then write books for a fee, telling you how they accomplished it. Knowledge is power, and at this time we know which group has the power.

Sisine was still trying to come up with another acceptable answer to her grandmother's question. Finally, she repeated her former answer by saying, "Well, he was a Black man with dreams."

"Girl, is that important?" shouted the surprised older lady, while the dumfounded younger woman still searched her brain for a more acceptable answer. The grandma smiled and focused her eyes, telling Sisine, "He founded the UNIA (United Negro Improvement Association) in 1911 with the aim of gaining economic, political, and military Equality for Black people with whites…he wanted to form a Black nation in Africa. They framed him for mail fraud in 1923, and sent him to prison for five years. He was released in 1927. Yes, you were right when you mentioned him as the forerunner to the great **Martin Luther King.**"

"Be careful of the forerunner description, you know. It almost sounds like John the Baptist and the Messiah," uttered a Knotted-dreadlocks, edging himself into the conversation.

"Are you a religious conservative, sir, or are you a political purist?" queried the witty matriarch.

"The I is apolitical at times," replied the Knotted One.

"Which time?"

"There is no hard and fast rule to the I political paradigm, loved one," replied the Knotted One as he high-stepped it on the tarmac and changed his luggage from one hand to the next.

"Political paradigm... loved one... Grandma...?" inquired the puzzled younger woman, shifting her gaze from the quiet matriarch to the lively Knotted One.

"Careful here with your patterns. Too many weird political patterns can be confusing to even the most brilliant mind."

"The I had known many main-stream dissidents in I days, but it is the first time the I hath come across an American woman of thy stature. The I even did like thee daugh-ta," replied the bearded one, looking studiously over his dark shades at the thin, wiry, strong-willed matriarch.

"Grandma, is he trying to date you?" asked the smiling younger woman.

"Are you asking me or asking him?"

"Well, he sounded different, but knowledgeable. He is kinda cute, too."

"Are you from here, sir," queried the matriarch, as she adjusted her wire-rimmed dark glasses for a better scrutiny of her new companion.

"Yes, but the I lived in your country for years." "And, practiced conservative religion?"

The Locks-One smiled saying, "The I's views are in conflict with the religious conservatives. They fought against changes, even in the days of slavery, so the I can't even did flex with them dis day.

Where are you staying here?"

"The hotel is called the Sea Breeze."

"Grandma, it is called the Sea Wind."

"Let the I show you around the place, with peace and love, man."

"Which one of the spellings? *Peace* or the other *piece*, sir?" replied the smiling matriarch.

"If we have to mix up our spellings, then we will just have to fix them up, too, Loved One."

"Loved One, again, Grandma! What are you guys really talking about?" inquired the puzzled granddaughter.

The sprightly matriarch and the Native One walked calmly along in a type of pregnant silence, giving each other slight lateral glances which really signals personal interests beyond the common social bonding, which draws them together as fellow travelers. This quiet personal assessment continued until the granddaughter broke the silence by shouting, "Now, we will have some good time!"

"About time for me," replied the matriarch.

"For all of us," acknowledged the Native One.

"Oh!" playfully moaned the Matriarchal One as she looked purposely at the smiling man who began to laugh in a low contented tone.

Mankin watched the drama being played out by these fellow passengers and mentally scripted many different scenarios of how their vacations might end. He knew they were of dissimilar backgrounds, ages, and even cultures, but it appears their agendas were similar. They were all interested in having happiness in their lives. They were all coming from a high-tech environment with its accommodating high stress and burnout syndrome. They were seeking some solace in a low-tech area where people choose to be human, and the pace of living slows down so that one can hear oneself think.

The Matriarch smiled at the mass of humanity that she encountered and loudly said, "This is truly a color reversal! Ha, ha. This really is fun. I am going to have some fun here."

"You are enjoying yourself Grandma?"

"Girl, I certainly am. In all my life I had never looked out in a crowd, and seen a mass of black with a sprinkling of white. I have always seen it the other way. The closest I have ever seen anything like this was the March on Washington."

"You were there during that event—the Washington March?"

"Yes, my Grandma was prominent during those times. She even talked with the great man, MLK," replied the beaming grandchild.

The "Knotted" native was tremendously impressed. He stopped dead in his tracks to openly admire this woman from his adopted country who had seen history in the making. She stopped, looked at him, and said in a low voice, "What is wrong now?"

The "Knotted-One" instantly lost his cultivated aloofness and even his natural mystique. He humbly walked up to the pretty, well manicured, but slightly perspiring woman, and quietly offered his hand in friendship, and in a gentle cultivated voice he said: "My name is Desmond. Lady what is your name?"

"My name is Tyrene, and my granddaughter's name is Sisine."

"It is an honor meeting you. Honestly, I mean it. Welcome to the land of my birth!"

"You certain you don't mean the land of the I birth," laughed the mischievous Sisine.

"Desmond, Sisine likes to build me up so be careful of her praising my past accomplishments."

"You mentioned earlier that you were going to have some fun. Yes, we are going to have some fun, and you are going to give me much more than fun. You are going to give me some firsthand information on how it was then. I actually have never met a real, true heroine. Matter of fact, everyone will have to meet you tonight. Thanks for visiting our island."

"What about me?"

"They will meet you also, Sisine."

The native son then shifted his luggage to his right hand, moved closer to his new-found friend, politely hugged her across the shoulder, slightly kissed the right side of her head nearest to her ear, and warmly muttered, "It is a great, warm, and spiritual feeling meeting you."

The composed matriarch met the challenge with great expertise. She lagged a half a step behind Desmond, then gently slipped her right arm around his waist as her pelvic region slightly caressed his left hip. She then acknowledged his attention by whispering, "I am deeply grateful for your compliment, Desmond. You are a person of great understanding." This action caught the subdued Desmond completely off his guard. He slightly stiffened his body to the cool touch of her small manicured fingers around his solar plexus. Before he could return control to his outer-self he looked at her. Their eyes met for a moment, and they both knew the translation was completed. As the small party carefully walked along the hot tarmac towards customs, the wily matriarch and the native son took small, evaluating glances at each other. Their timely, physically organized bumping into each other and their tactful apologies just brought smiles to each others' faces. They knew they had to keep alive their conversation to enliven their newfound friendship while waiting in the slow and boring customs line. Each now pondered what next to say. The Knotted One broke the embarrassing silence with a religious statement.

"You asked before if I am a religious conservative or a political purist. I am a scientific person who has recognized the limitations of scientific knowledge in our everyday life."

"I think you were Dreadlocks, or the other one, the one from the UNIA. How come you are now calling yourself otherwise?"

"Does the hair make a difference, lady?"

"No!"

"Grandma wants to know if you are a Dreadlocks or the Rastafarian type."

"I am who I am—a human being who will not be labeled otherwise. I believe in truth, and if either one is truth, then I am that. Would 'Bald-head' make a difference?" laughed the Knotted One, knowing that neither woman got the joke.

"Why the joke, sir?" asked a puzzled matriarch. "I have nothing against bald-headed people."

The Knotted One and the ingenious matriarch exchanged meaningful smiles. "Remind me to tell you that 'Bald head' here means otherwise."

"You mean bald head is not bald head here?" questioned Sisine, shaking her head in mild disbelief. "I wonder what else is different. Well, …"

"Well, it seems we have much to learn here, Sisine. Now, this good gentleman is telling us we will be re-educated; possibly with some of his scientific and spiritual values. Am I right, sir?"

"Grandma, it sounds like we are going back to school here."

"Life in itself is a school, Sisine," mentioned the Knotted one.

"Then let's pray together for social and spiritual equity," laughed a jubilant Tyrene.

"Can I, too, pray with you all for whatever is good? It seems I am the lonely one without a companion in this group. No one seems to like little ole me anymore," mocked a smiling Sisine, as she put her hand on her forehead in feinted lamentation.

"Sisine, let's form a spiritual trio," said Desmond.

"Like Mr. Spock said, 'we are one,'" replied a laughing Sisine.

"Cooperation will get us everywhere, and love makes it easy," replied Tyrene.

"Grandma, who is that man winking at?"

"Let's guess!"

"Pray tell me, dear Sisine," roared the Desmond with gusto.
"Life is a summation of experiences, dear daughter."

"A what?" replied the smiling Sisine, looking askance at the winking young man.

As Mankin listened to the travelers, he thought about religion and science in our everyday life. He knew that the study of science tries to give a quantified explanation to all things in our lives. Then again all things are not tangible. The use of statistics, probabilities, and other mathematical constructs are useless as measuring sticks for these personal qualities. The human experience goes beyond business and logical ego constructs. We are not really logical beings; we are more spiritual beings playing in a physical world where physical things are everyday manifestations. At this time, it appears it is easier to be physical **than spiritual**. The gateway to human satisfaction is the inner zone where we are truly happy with all of life's experiences. For this to happen, there are no pure numbers or empiricist formulas. We all are unique, but we have a tendency to dance to different sounds from the same "creative drum." As the old saying goes, "What is one man's meat is another man's poison." Oh yes, that means woman, too.

The enemy of science is uncertainty. Uncertainty is very annoying in this scientific age when everyone is concerned with reaching decisions in predictable fashions. We want the certainty of science. On the opposite side, people view ambiguity and uncertainty (guesswork) as the enemy of science. This causes scientific knowledge to be regarded as power, whereas the lack of such knowledge is seen as impotence! Prayer does not exhibit the same predictability as science. As a matter of fact, if time is of the essence, and as mortality is predictable but the definite time is unknown, so prayers may be predictable, but we are too temporary to see their fulfillment. Our present problem is we want it now! Perhaps we feel we have been waiting forever to get our just rewards. Are we tired of waiting for deliverance by an outside messiah? Tired of listening to the business-minded conglomerates of *tel-evangelist*-types harangue us on how to "buy" into Eternity (for a fee of course.) Is this similar to the Roman Catholic business concept of purgatory, in openly showing more interests in power and money than in piety? Anyway, living with only the scientific concept is like purging the spirit and accepting only the technological solution—traveling the road to becoming an automaton.

Most of the time, the migrants' preachers' claim of seeing things from a spiritual perspective is just an accommodation to gain more dollars, and some cents, because so many of their congregation refuse to exhibit common sense. Everyone needs to practice a more realistic view of spirituality—to seek a more accommodating world beyond the senses.

One can't demand the Spirit to do anything; one has to invite its help. It is unconscionable, hearing screaming church leader-types who stand for nothing and embrace everything where money is concerned, telling migrant congregations that they *will* the Spiritual Essence to give them abundance. Today, we have to pay these intolerant sociological preachers before they will give us the word. These professional preachers will not be enticed to appear without knowing the quantity of people present. Quantity of cash is proportional to number of congregates. Cool marketing strategy—heavy, free-market strategy. Oh, let's check the stock market to see which Christian preaching cartel is doing well today... Oh, no we can't see them! They are being camouflaged by a nesting of shadowy holding companies. Beware of **the super (religious + political)** immigrant leaders who get into some new, and complex, religious fantasy land with blaring synthesizers and high-power addressing systems to draw more people to their meetings. The noise decibel is higher, but the spiritual content decreases with the noise volume. Some preachers even change religions, expecting to have more inner peace (equating this with having more money). They will be appeased momentarily, but the novelty soon wanes...and crash! An advice to the migrant—go beyond a desire to please or praise the preacher or his social theocratic (or political) hierarchy. Migrants, move away from the past perception where the preacher knows it all, and step into a more spiritually inclined present-day reality. When the noisy show is over, you will still have to deal with the TRUTH!

Most of the time, the immigrants are thinking about magic (trick) as a quick fix instead of miracles, which are the work of faith. Mankin knew that religion divides people into little controlled groups, but spirituality empowers people by bonding them together in a true understanding of faith. The migrants' addiction to these showy religious leadership-types generally led to abuse of their family and placing their social stratification into a permanent underclass (masses). This is very noticeable among women who are the matriarch of the family. It is no wonder that most preachers' messages are directed at women with an emphasis that they should obey men, the leaders of the flock of course! (An alpha-wolf with numerous unsupported illegitimate children...a real *father of the nation,* too.) There are so many immigrants who have failed to do well, because they buried themselves into these unhealthy religious practices. They are inclined to listen to people momentarily soothing them, and their young ones, with messages that condemn them to ignorance, and therefore, servility. Let's stop having preachers mislead us with their massive, misinterpreted messages as they fill their coffers with our hard-earned cash. They dress in these silly-looking, ritualistic gowns, "telling us who we are not," while peddling their doctrine of imaginary euphoria that is strictly tied to the amount of your donation to their collection plates. They are always taking without giving any concerns for the development of our young. They even have the audacity to be preaching against women and sex, while holding out their greedy hands for cash. We are still waiting for them to give us an Earthly partner that is better than woman and sex. They are acting as if they can do better than the Creator. Show us your new design. Wake up. You can't buy heaven!   As one distraught and annoyed immigrant lady confronted her preacher, implying that if CHRIST is so much against women and female sexuality, then there must be a **Christ**ine some place that will understand her and all women who need understanding in being a female. The wily preacher abruptly changed direction telling her, "Men are unjust, and you don't know whom to trust…" She smiled in agreement, tactfully asking him if he was a man. We need true knowledge and faith so as not to be tied to some of the babble being sold by these preachers, shouting at us for a price. The price is too high, especially in a community where information is at a premium among poor immigrants. Has anyone recently observed the behaviors of the Caribbean preachers? They have adopted the new North American preaching style of shouting, screaming, and giving a show. Why not? They are following the Christian Bible in this case. "When you go to Rome, do as the Romans do." Did someone say this is North America? Don't get carried away with geography here. Shift! **"Can I have a witness (for a price)?"**

Religion is really a person's inner self, an experience of individual truth. (But first, be warned here; they kill people for telling the TRUTH!) Unfortunately, most religions tend to emphasize sect and dogma instead of the inner truth. They seem more apt to address the intellect instead of the soul. Their dogmas fix us into little cubicles, like psychotic gang members wearing colors to signify their affiliations. Truly, without religion, the human spirit would go into decay, but without science, humanity may be unaware of this decay. We need our inner self to be dynamic, pure, and happy. So let's have both science and prayer in our daily lives. Yes, Tyrene was correct, "we are a summation of our experiences."

Mankin can still remember being asked by a very close friend: "Why should a believer have people from other religions come to speak at their church? Are these members still searching for something to believe in?"

"Wait! Don't all religious paths lead to only one point—to the Creator, GOD?"

My friend, perhaps, has not paid much attention to the saying; "knowledge is power." No wonder so many atrocities have been committed in the name of God. The religious leaders are political disrupters instead of spiritual soul sustainers. The immigrants need to put some worthwhile decision in their lives. As the spiritualists sometimes say, "This does not means libido over church credo (i. e. your erotic desires over church credence)." Choose your own partner by yourself. Make your own decisions, or at least be part of the decision-making process, not the institutional result. We know many people who previously made what they considered a wrong choice, especially when choosing mates. It seems the "pervasive" view among divorced church people (women especially) is that they personally choose their mate without Jesus the Christ's permission. This, they believe, caused their divorce. It appears some people are just escapists who refuse to take their share of the blame for anything. They want to blame their Creator for any problem that may befall them, saying he created the World and its obstacles. Now, these congregants claim they are waiting for Jesus Himself to send them a mate! Well, with GOD, all things are possible—but tick-tock, tick-tock—don't miss decision time.

People need to take their freedom from these institutionalized religions with their "intellectual old-boy club" leadership. They are always dictating policy to the downtrodden, but they never actually fight for a spiritual homogeneity for all people. The human experience needs a more eclectic approach to stimulate happiness and understanding among the various groups, especially so in a rapidly changing world. The exclusionary attitude of the entrenched religious leadership (masculine privileges), which are structured along gender lines will not last in the face of the present-day female awareness. There is an entrenched feeling against "women preachers," especially in most ethnically controlled churches. What are these men really afraid of? Their mothers? Or, women in general? Could it be that they are intimidated by the innate persuasive powers of the females to cut into their money racket if they are given a preaching chance? "Just give them a chance, and it will be the end of us all…they brought us here, and they have the power to send us back, too…" Laugh. These preacher-types certainly failed their people. Why not give the other gender a chance? Do you think they will do better and replace you? Or, do they think women will do worse? "Do you think she is going to whip you as Mom did, my son!" If Mom whipped you, that was a long time ago. At least we hope so! Now, grow up and listen to the Word. To refuse women leadership is to lose a sense of love. The world is full of these awful religious frauds, always trying to be the Masters. There are many powerless, short-sighted men, trying to cling to their silly imaginary power base. It is so pathetic to hear their jaded sermons on the "evils of sex." If sex is so evil, why are they always craving it! Why even get married then, Mr. Preacher? In their dealings with the politicians, they lost the insight to preach righteousness; they seek popularity and share power on a temporal plane. In reality, most preachers are just political animals with a penchant for misinterpretation of the scriptures for political gains. Is it true that even the Devil can quote the sacred text? As one **Rastafarite commented,** "The plastic preachers hid their deeds by taking comfort in the "condom culture." The "bagging up and throwing away of their seeds," hiding from the public their misdeeds while they continued lying about the pleasures of sex as they continued mistreating the queens in their congregations." Really, Mr. Nyah-man, thou hath observed that, too? How about churches that still believed their racially mixed congregations should have a division of power-sharing along racial lines. Guess which hue the menial helpers are? Yes, those who are strictly forbidden to wear braids, because it is equated with a demon emblem from darkest Africa! Is it really? Now, enlighten us as to why these immigrants still attend these congregations. Is it the "making of a joyful noise," or are they afraid to displease the powerful offering-taking "messenger" in his flowing white robe who is always pointing to the white suffering icon on a cross. Now, one has to consider if it is sheer coincidence that the displayed *suffering-icon-on-the-cross* and the *offering-taking-messenger'* is of the same shade! The immigrants are more concerned about his theatrical shouting and pointing techniques than they are about the message. Could it be these migrant women believe this message of their African ancestral inferiority and demon possession? (Yes, yes, we all know the majority of them believe in *duppys*, ghosts, and *rolling calves,* but let's get on with the story about the spiritless preachers.) Imagine a church full of immigrant female sheep, preaching against Black women while shackling them to the rigid rules of giving their hard earned cash to the collection plate. What do these women tell their daughters and sons who attend these places? "Children obey your masters!" By the way, this type of exclusionary attitude is even more rampant in many ethnic churches. When will the immigrants, especially the women, ever learn to avoid congregations where these supremacists reign. Oh, by the way, many women help these men to perpetuate this dominance against other women through personal dislike or "pillow politics" (decision?). Is it time now to take a stand, and go beyond the rituals and the cool, showy rhetoric?

Looking through the bus window, Mankin observed the changes in the city's infrastructure. He mentally compared them to bygone days of colonial rule when things were moving at a slower pace, and possibly, were a bit more orderly. He tried with an objective rationale to decide if things were orderly or not. Perhaps there were comparable crimes, but the smaller population then gave the impression that things were calmer. On the other hand perhaps people were less outspoken about injustice. There were certainly injustices; however, they would not reach the timid newspaper editors or be discussed by the leaders of the institutionalized churches, whose main concern was to not "rock the boat" but be properly attired in their ceremonial garbs at military parades and functions. Monkey see, monkey do! They are copycats of their colonial masters. As he takes in the view, he wonders if the country was going through a period of social malaise or experiencing growing pains. His inner self silently queried his outer vision with the question, "What's the difference?"

Mankin smiled to himself as he found himself voicing an opinion. "Are we losing it? Who is in charge here, now?" This exchange was not meant as relative to the changing geopolitical structure of the society but as a centering signal to the inner self to be objective in the evaluation of the present society to the past generation. It is very difficult to be objective when your generation is being evaluated with the present one. The mind cannot be neutral, so it continually fights for a decision, which is, or was, comfortable to its knowledge. The colonial times were the era it knew well. It was not a dynamic time of growth or opportunities. It was a time of make believe grandeur for toothless colonial masters, whose prime had long past. A time of less social complexity, especially when seen through younger eyes with minimal obligations. A period when there was a great zest for knowledge. A time when all positive behaviors were still considered to emanate only from a non-Black hue. Well, has that changed since then? You tell me to what extent. If you cannot remember, ask yourself about the law that allows the police to arrest poor people found in up-scale neighborhoods on a charge of vagrancy. Did Mankin shock you? Or, are you shocked by rather not remembering "the good old days?" There was no information, then, on inhumane treatments in the prison or otherwise; no social activist could survive in those days. Rule Britannia, but you will not wash away the waves of injustice perpetuated on poor **defenseless people! This brings to mind** one of Her Majesty's former unwilling occupants, "Son-Son Mighty" who usually tells tales of these social conditions in prison. He claimed that after his release, he was so upset that he broke into the prison one night and re-possessed his usual tools. Imagine an upset ex-inmate breaking into a prison to *liberate* his usual farm tools. Well, freedom is freedom, and if everything is spiritually linked, then inanimate objects need freedom too. Perhaps, just perhaps this could have been "Son-Son Mighty's" reasoning before selling those tools! They possibly needed a kinder and gentler owner than the English monarch.

Mankin remembered, too well, seeing, on a cool bleak morning, one of the last icons of the colonial masters as he ambled on three legs down the whitewashed Parade Square, with its circular concrete streets enclosed with dark wrought iron fences. "The icon," with his air of cultivated British jocularity, smiled proudly as he put some smoke in his lungs as if to proclaim, "We are one Empire forever!" He then turned the corner of the Square, walked to musty old naval monument, and then was gone. Like his Empire? The next day a school friend wrote:

I know churches

I have seen hills

I also have seen Churchill!

He ambles across the Square, looking amicable in a
child's view

Yes, once a man, twice a child

The last vestige of jolly ole England passed before mine
eyes

under his own volition, but on three legs?

But with belabored breath as he scanned the gathering
of subjected foreigners

who came out to observe an icon of foreign imperialism

Hopefully the last trace of the patriarchal bosses

He vanished around the edge of the circular Square;
never to be seen again.

They left on the cold and bleak morn

Thanks!

      For what?

The faces changed since a young friend wrote this, but it appears the struggle takes on a different shade and diversification. Are the politicians, now, doing a better job with the resources they have? Are they trying to make life better for their people? It seems there are plenty here for all of us to be satisfied; so, why the scarcity? Are we standing waist deep in water and still dying of thirst? Looking around, Mankin has to believe the saying that, "poverty is man made." It has nothing to do with nature (when seen from these national perspectives!) Everyone here seems to believe he or she is a superstar doing the "moon walk." They dress the part, but cannot sustain the "strut" due to their lack of cash—the American dollars. Where are the agriculture-based people, the farmers? Prices are astronomically high here; way beyond the moon, where most aspiring "moon-**walkers**" cannot tread. **Begging,** with lack of self-respect, is rampant. People seem to adopt the worst social characteristics of North America in using the ghetto slang and mannerisms to do their communications. The returning immigrants reinforce most of these types of behaviors, not just by the displaced and often despicable "deportees" who seems to bear the brunt of all negative events in these communities. The populace blamed the "deportees" for all criminal affairs, reminding one of the simple habits of formerly blaming "ghosts" and the Devil for every unhappy event. There is a serious hustle here to make ends meet.

On a bustling narrow street, smiling peddlers showed their wares to visitors with quiet dignity. This new behavior showed governmental training had improved the primitive din of their past hawk-and-peddling. Mankin marveled at the controlled, jovial display of these sellers (higglers) with the orderly exchange of goods and money. He remembered in the past when noisiness and a type of organized confusion was the order of the day. Mankin recalled the incident between a fierce hard-core street pseudo-rasta, (often called pork-rasta, but of course, not to his face!) and a noisy and dominant, unsmiling city higgler in another market square. Here one has to remember there is not much obedience to the rules of civility among these two groups. Now, some higglers have a tendency to belch loudly, claiming they are relieving "gas" from their stomach. The general excuse is, "Mi never drink mi tea this morning." This higgler was using the same excuse as she uttered outrageous belches while rubbing her stomach area. The "rasta" immediately looked at her and loudly exclaimed that if her "*gas*" had changed in a downward direction, it certainly would have blown off her "clothes." One can just imagine the ensuing verbal fracas! Words... "Ole gal, think you ah some *expletive* iron-chewing grass-yard Gongalee. Boy, go way you mi-yacka-mi-yacka, puttu putta *expletive* pork-eating rasta you. Think you ah roll thunder. Move and go bathe; think a mi, and you a wrap up in a crocus bag a night time." Belch! "I agree, you alone a wrap up in a your crocus bag...ugly meager, dry foot pi-yacka pi-yacka, gal, mi have a bed!"

At least those conditions had never stopped commercial transaction, although they stopped many buyers from visiting these market sellers because of the sellers' attitudes. Well Mankin chalked up one for modernity. He knew he preferred the present type of commercial atmosphere. He knew the sellers still have the same acrid tongues, especially if they felt a bit slighted. **In this** precarious world, one feels like dangling on a tight rope between the modern socially re-engineered attitudes of the new Free-Marketism and the deep-rooted entrenched cultural vibrancy of simple viragoism. In this, their "higgler's world," everyone tries to be the ruler on the block. How can Mankin ever forget that dreaded, but showy higgler who wanted to change her street name from "The Bull" to Jezebel Janko. Everyone tells her she is testing fate, because no one is ever again named Jezebel or Judas (at least not openly or officially). She wanted this name because another competitor's friend is called John Crow Pickney! Well everyone has their trademark, and in her area, the most outlandish name carries weight, even within her church clique, too. When her friends in the choir decided to call her Jezebel Janko, her pastor was shocked. He tactfully explained to her that people already loved her dearly, and possibly, they were afraid of her, too, although she is a lovely and a desirous lady. Which she was of course. When he told her that others might not want to be with her if her name was changed, she immediately asked for their names so that she could "...lick dem in a dem...!" This lady, The Bull, never had her wish, because common sense and the status quo (perhaps even superstition, too) prevailed. As Mankin time-traveled through this episode, wondering what's in a name, he noticed a very serious-looking, well-dressed woman approach a seller and defiantly ask, "How much for your water coconut?"

"Twenty five dollars."

"Are you damn crazy, or do you think I am a fool or just arrived?"

"Lady, I have to make a profit, too. I bought it from someone else."

"Tell me anything. You all want to make big houses off people. Blasted thieves, you all are. You and your *cumbolo* must have thieved it from your friends!"

Wrong choice of words—it's not culturally acceptable to be called a thief. Armageddon time—step away from the thin veneer of social facade, back to the natural basic cultural viragoism. War!!!

"What! You over-painted, unnatural smelling baboon. Who are you calling thief? If you can't pay the price, why don't you get back in your car, and stop telling people how to run their business. You bandy-legged calf," shouted the seller as she shifted to an easier position in her small wicker chair.

"Wait, a whom the piss-pot smelling, donkey-faced, moldy-frocked gal talking to?" retorted the serious-faced, well-dressed buyer as she stopped and looked the seller up and down with studied disdain.

"Look, woman, don't make me have to be rude to you. Ahem."

"You rude to me already by calling me a thief."

"You know very well I don't mean you are a thief."

"Most of you go away and come back, trying to treat us like dogs. We may not have all your fine clothes, or walk like 'John Crow a step on bun grun,' but we have pride."

"Den nuh so," muttered the crowd in unison, with support for their seller friend.

"Come, come now. Just stop right there. Did you send me anywhere? Don't give me any of your bloody rubbish about 'come back.' Come back from where?"

"We nuh fool; we all know you travel. A try to show off on us. We nuh grudge you for your good looks, your money, or appearance."

"Or my 'John Crow bun-grun-walking'?" replied the nattily dressed woman, in a more composed attitude.

"Look ma, cuss cuss nuh have good word."

"Look, lady, my mother was a higgler, and I know the ropes; so, no body is going to verbally 'draw and quarter me' in the streets in the market square. As for my 'bun grun walking,' my lover likes it. If you have it, use it as the saying goes."

"Yes, ma, you pretty, educated, young, and have lots of rhythm, but you don't have to treat me bad because I am a poor old woman."

"Don't give me any of your poor higgler rubbish. I told you before I know the ropes. If you have children, I am certain they are at some Ivy League college in the States or possibly Oxford or Cambridge in England. You own properties here, live in some big mansion, and have never paid taxes. Another thing, you are a young woman. If you were an old person, I would have let everything slide and just walked away."

"You know what, take the water coconut for free, because you are trying to have the government look in a mi taxes. Mi, a poor Christian woman, am just trying to make a living to overcome hardship."

"You are a poor woman? If you want to pretend poor, then remove your $500 diamond earrings!"

The seller's hands immediately flew to her ears like someone removing their hands from a hot stove. She gave a broad satisfied smile and flaunted her body in a sexually suggestive way, which defines a social status in the seller's hierarchy. Her friends started touching their earlobes in silence, amid guarded whispers and sighs as they shot envious glances at their silent companion who pretended to be unaware of the commotion she caused. She was actually enjoying every moment of her triumph.

"I will pay for your coconut, lady. Boy, things are expensive everywhere."

"I would make you a present, but if you insist."

"Here is your money. Thanks."

"Thelma!" shouted a Caucasian-looking young woman.

"Vivian, what are you doing here? I thought you were in London," answered the neatly dressed customer.

"Do you know this lady?" asked the seller.

"Yes she is my roommate in college. She took care of me all those years in college when I was sick."

"Well, well" said the seller with an embarrassing smile creasing the side of her mouth. "My daughter's roommate and me (or is it, and I?) have been properly introduced in the market square."

The seller then reached down deep into her "thread bag" purse and said, "Miss Thelma, here is your money for the coconut. It was meant to be free anyway."

"I am sorry about what I said to you. Are you giving me the coconut because you are a Christian?"

"Who is a Christian?" exclaimed Vivian.

"Ha! Ha! Pickni unoo nuh give mi nuh trouble, yah."

"You and mom had a fight out here?"

"She is your mother?"

"Yes!"

"Oh, my gosh. I am very sorry about this whole event."

"Lawd ma, you have to learn to hold your own in this world. This is woman time. Sometime you have fi take no prisoner. Nuh act like you a 'quashie.' If you 'fraid of eyes, you can't eat head. Be bold and knowledgeable, ma."

Mankin raised his brow and silently walked away, thinking how funny things happened everywhere, especially in the market square, here, where people tend to be very basic, and the spirit is less fettered with high tone civility. As someone once said, "There is no coincidental occurrence. Events are all planned and happened in allotted time frames of references." These players all have a common link—the market place. We are all linked, and nothing can change that. The link seems to be more intensified (or more personalized) in smaller communities. Perhaps this loss of personal touch causes the stress that seems to pervade the industrial countries. On the other hand, this personalized attention can distract your attention to just simple and mundane things, putting you in a simple mode of gross irresponsibility. Well, enjoy it while it lasts, because if it is enjoyable, the politicians and their free-market friends will certainly find a way to make it illegal or taxable.

POLITICIANS

Recently the politicians in these islands jumped on the free-market bandwagon using a North American-type media blitz to propagandize their constituencies. Now, one has to pity any media person going into an area to conduct an interview without notifying the Member of Parliament (MP) of that area. It seems the media is required to notify the MP so he or she can prepare one of those "make me look good" responses. Talking about (mis)managing the news. Do you think the media would go along with this? Definitely, they are always wish-washy anyway. Politicians, here, have problems reaching a consensus on even the simplest advantageous thing for their nation. Because of this, they committed themselves to **Political flagellation of** beating the nation to death with visionless policies, due to lack of nationalistic pride, moral integrity, and their own narcissism. No wonder Mankin's friend Willout thinks the emerging states are all one-party states. They all voted on the party line, even for the most asinine issue. It seems here that the government's number one priority is retaining power and disagreeing with the opposition. There is no consensus!

Mankin looked through the local newspaper and was shocked to see how ineffective the local politicians were. They tried to play God but were unwilling to be crucified by the people, which is contrary to the "god-like" qualities. Actually, they were the ones doing the crucifixion with high prices and a tendency to sell out the people's future to foreigners, waving big bank-rolls and espousing the tired 1990s proclamation of the "free enterprise system." They have not learned much from the 1970s, when the interests of the country were sold out by the "ethnic commercial few" who controlled the majority. The view that big business is the soul and spirit of a country needs to be reviewed on a global scale. Business may be the tool that runs an enterprise, a country, or whatever, but the spirit and soul of any country are the human resources who are willing to cooperate for the betterment of humanity. Historically, there were always businesses, and humanity was never better off then. How about human chattel slavery? How about slavery and Apartheid South Africa where their political structure was maintained by the "free" enterprise businesses in the USA and Europe (especially the UK)? This was done with the connivance of their subsidiary, the United Nations. Can you believe that over all those years the UN could not free Namibia from the clutches of South Africa?

The treatment of Zimbabwe, Mozambique, Namibia, Angola, and the Sharpeville Murders (not *incident*, please! It was murder which took place with the big powers looking on.) How can anyone from that time ever forget the picture of a young African leader in tears, pleading with a British colonial master for intercession on behalf of the poor and helpless people in South Africa? The arrogant, unfeeling Briton refused with the pompous remarks that it took some asinine large quantity of logistics to help the "natives." He even derided the question by asking if that African leader was willing to lead the army to fight the South Africans. Perhaps he was still angry with the Mau Mau (not the Egyptian cat) of Kenya for seeking parity with the oppressors. Has anyone ever really asked where was the United Nations then? Sometimes people wonder if the oppressed people in South Africa remember those murdered and the names of their murderers. **No trial at Nuremberg, eh?** Notice that when people of a certain hue are being slaughtered, the ever so vigilant UN takes time out for a light beer. No, they would not order dark beer. The beer color might remind them of coagulating blood, resulting in nausea. We cannot have a conflict of conscience, because the next time they may want to do the correct thing—not the political thing. Remember the Rwanda killings? Now, it was a little different where the murderers and the UN "Biggie" was of the same hue. Is there a lesson here? Not a genocide, eh! Let's just try to determine the UN's definition of genocide— "The killing of a certain quantity of people of a specific hue, with the necessary resources that are desired by the Western World."

It appears war criminals are people who lost wars after killing certain types of people. If not, how come no one in South Africa or the old Ian Smith's Rhodesia was ever tried as a war criminal? Could it be because they had powerful Western contacts?

Some of these politicians here are as helpful as using gargoyles in the front of parliament buildings to scare away evil spirits. If these gargoyles were effective, many of the elected politicians would not be able to enter Parliament. They turned Parliament into a place where jackasses are enthroned and rule supreme for what seems like eternity. It is one thing to tolerate wishy-washy politicians, but it is quite another to ask us to accept their policies with no vision or optimism of change—a kind of visionless agenda. They have the type of benefit packages that are diluted beyond usefulness with trivialities. All politicians play popularity games, but these here are actually pompous little buffoons who really started believing their own press releases. There are politicians (let's call them nationalists, because statesmen is not a true description, since many of these stalwarts are women) who have some spirit and willingness to make beneficial changes. Alas, too few. Let's not forget the last **woman** who challenged the System and patriarchal boss, **The Chief,** who is rumored to have said, "Those who are with me can eat and drink at the table over there. Those that are not with me will have to leave the

Party!" He meant to leave his political party. All the men rushed to the table. A lone woman stood her ground with inner conviction defiantly against the spineless cadre of male quasi politicians to face an exclusionary judgment. Those were simpler days when a politician could show her "undies" purporting that the opponent's wife could not wear those attractive types! Simple, but very effective. No need for guns to enforce the point.

Anyway, the politicians usually have their way. Or, more correctly, always have their say, which is generally verbiage to appease the masses. One of these were overheard saying: "You all go away and come back with these grandiose schemes, trying to tell us what to do. You are all copycats trying to write about our problems from your ivory towered academic hilltops. You think you know about us, but you don't. If you are dissatisfied with our system, just don't think to eliminate those in power, first think how to effectively supplant them with effective leadership to avoid chaos." Telling us what to do! What? Wake up. There are no 'them and us.' There are only us. We are you, and you are we; can't you understand that yet? No wonder there is a feeling that we are at war with each other. If you do not understand that there is no "them or us," just try understanding immigrants who have problems with the legal system. They, too, had believed that they were better than their fellow immigrants from a different country. They would hold this belief that their country was superior until the System overseas re-educated them that they are similar to the demonized Black "social-enemy-types" with no special endearing quality. This is the "they" and the "we" that prevails in most immigrant society, especially in the island mentality that has caused a strong division among its people Overseas. The deadly result of this destructive tribal trend leads to "Garrison politics" on their islands and the rise and continuity of the ferocious gunmen.

Really, these guys' policies are formulated and implemented for them (for us all) in Washington. No problem there, but talking about "telling them what to do" is a farce. Is someone singing, "What have you done for me lately?" Better wake-up, island politicians, or the Foreign 'Rulers' will destroy us separately or equally—together as one. There would be more of us to destroy as one, especially with the population explosion taking place on these islands.

Politicians need a contract with humanity, not a contract on the powerless masses. The new Overseas political tendency is to cut social security and raise taxes on the poor (Of course we know the rich are always in a tax-avoidance mode.) to ensure more riches reach the pockets of the elite. The immigrants have seen the recent political changes, where all parties succumb to the ultra-right wing rhetoric that preach hate and disenfranchisement of people of color (foreigners). Do people really need this type of clinical machinery leadership, or do they need a more humane grass-roots one? Recently, many conservative politicians are advertising their virtue as the ability to kill others. What about: "I asked for the death penalty in most of my cases. Vote for me, and I will get the death penalty for you!" Be careful here; they mean it. Have you notice they never mentioned anything concerning guilt? Ever try finding out why they want to get the death penalty *for* you? Did you ask them to get it for you? Perhaps they want it for themselves. Have you ever looked at the faces of those they want to give the death penalty? Just remember this, "the same knife that **kills** goat will kill sheep, too!" There is something absolutely wrong when aspiring rulers scream at us on television to choose them because of their capability as killers of humanity. Are there other living issues too?

Now, even the most sensitive politician sees justice for migrants as a liability to winning. Justice takes a backseat, as the migrants become expendable in the race for political popularity. As politicians jockey for winning political favors and towing the "party-line," the immigrants suffer political disenfranchisement. More so, too, because immigrants have a tendency not to vote on any issue. They will whine later at the results, but they certainly are not activists; so they paid the price! They fail to understand the media usage of "voter manipulation" by shaping public opinion against them. They do not seem to see welfare bashing and the excessive painting of criminals as part of the immigrant groups as threats to their social acceptance.

Recent political strategy tries to prove prosperity depends only on individual self-reliance and not on constant handouts from an interfering state institution. This is manipulating the politics of resentment—the new political folly—to first preach fiscal prudence by bashing the poor before abandoning them. For this, they find a receptive audience in the lower-middle class and other right-wing fringe groups. Conservatives now advocate unbounded free enterprise and free trade and the elimination of government regulations and social welfare. (How about committing crime but not going to prison? Is that next?) These popular right-wing economic theories are strategies for the **alienation of the poor** after the fall of communism. It seems that the Western economy was built on a war against communism, and the demise of communism has caused economic hardships. As the politicians embrace the new free-market system and abdicate their responsibility, we all seem to be headed for mass poverty and environmental degradation. It appears that the conservative right-wing believe in the power of the free-market system to solve all social dilemmas. Remember, they had believed in chattel slavery (and elitism) also! Perhaps they still do. Free market is great for generating wealth (economic growth), but it is not a cure-all for a just and civilized society where human values predominate. There must be some government control/oversight to balance income inequality and not just for passing laws that single out the poor/needy for punishment, because they did not measure up to the new norms of affluence. We are now living in a society where government has conceded its roles of governing, the promotion of social equity, and the control of corporate excesses. The elected officials are now too prone to give into the corporate demands of the free-market system. The government foolishly bowed to the demands of foreign developers by destroying the environment—bird sanctuaries and other reserves—for the promises of mere pittance as return for their cooperation. We are all guilty, as individuals, because in most of these small countries the populace turns a blind eye to the pillages. Their excuse is that we need more jobs. Truthfully, many times the governments of these small states have no recourse but to implement draconian policies which are dictated by the Great Overload States. Small states are unable to stand up to theses "giants" who sabotage their independence by undermining loan approvals that are necessary for the survival of the poor smaller states. They are generally forced by the Overlord States to sign "papers" that undermine their sovereignty just to stay ahead of total instability. In the last struggle for signing what is referred to as a "Ship Rider" agreement, we see the poor verbally defending themselves against the rich. Their defense can only be verbal, as history has so often shown! Yes, who would hear us when we scream? Does the Gravey's Doctrine come to mind here? It appears the Oppressed group had an apocalyptic destiny with the sea. Ships took them to Western slavery, and ships were again used to control their growth. One has to remember that there is nothing that small and weak countries can do; food comes before policies. Someone once mentioned that "economic reality dictates political policy." That is still true, but sometime policy is pure dishonesty. Never forget the "golden rule" that those with the gold make the rule.

We are in a world of pretense, where imagery reigns, and substance evaporates into that nebulous chasm between smooth rhetoric and cold realism. We sometime feel we are staying in a system which induces "living fatigue" —a hopeless state where there is nothing to look forward to except taxes and surging bureaucratic pressures. In this relentless war of attrition of spiritual values, the elite with their myriad of technocrats used the media and public relation gurus to brain wash the public about their virtues of helping humanity to live a better life. The immigrants tend to believe these constructed scenarios of hypothetical benefits, which are really double talk to confuse the masses into service with little pay and to get ineffective politicians re-elected for numerous terms. Government no longer considers better social programs or more jobs. The newfound priority is international market speculation; people priorities seem to no longer count! Now, international money speculators from the Overlord Powers rob small countries of their economic independence, and therefore, their sovereignty. These speculators use excessively intricate, risky, short-term speculative tactics— a type of grab and flee (Or, is it RAF, rob and flee?) plan to suck out the every iota of strength from these regions. There is, now, no further need for the usual military incursion, because international financial speculators can effectively rob government of its power to govern by using their glib-tongued "economists" to mesmerize small countries with their empty promises. No wonder economists and their money-manager friends are considered the "confusers" of this world. Have you ever listened to these guys' predictions?

"Upturns, downturns, bullish markets, seasonal fluctuation due to drying up of the dollars in the Asiatic Basin, new highs, new lows, corrective curve to firm up the market, moving away from shaky grounds (Is he expecting an earthquake?), putting some *fun*ds in a *broke*-(age) area (Who wants to be broke for the ages? That would be no fun!), a dollar holdup makes it more attractive (Is he talking about a certain type of robbery?), stock driving index, manipulate the curve straight into a downstream to straighten out the tail end of the spin (Woe, this sounds like some dizzy "head-tripping," mach-3 ride here. Is this like saying his straight line is a circle? If so, then, when will our question mark becomes an exclamation point?), cap an index fund, create a portfolio, etc.

After all this cloaked speculative rambling, he finally tells us, "You are going to be either 'standard' or 'poor!'" Is this practical or mythical? Now, we need another expert to decipher his predictions. Please don't ask—he *will* recommend one of his friends!

Believe it or not, these are the high-profile-types of predictors that governments have to deal with when they do business with financial institutions. They even "advise" these small nations how to spend "wisely." Frightening, isn't it? The government must realize that business people are not generally known for their fight for social justice. "Free traders" are business people, too. Are we experiencing very slow erosion of the elected officials' willingness to help the people? A type of erosion that ends in death of elected government? Is this the time when we look to the local warlords for help, because the elected officials have left the premises and abnegated their responsibilities after the election? It is a known fact that politics is issue-oriented rather than feeling-specific (or spiritually inclined), but how does one totally remove one's feeling to another place when misery continually confronts one? Did someone mention that dictators "blessed" by these Overlords oversee this type of human degradation every day? Some of these poor small sovereign (?) states even export their short-sightedness in political savvy when it comes to defending the rights of their own citizens in foreign lands. For example, farm workers complain many times about inhumane conditions on overseas farms. Their government representatives are so politically emasculated that they refuse to do anything to help the farmers. If these farm workers choose to join a union overseas to correct this inhumane treatment, then their own government at home threatens them with prosecution. When we realize that people from the host country can join the union and demand better working conditions, whereas imported workers are barred from doing so by their own government. This cause one to question the type of message such a country is sending to the world— "Our workers will work under inhumane conditions for a few cents."

Is this slavery, again, or what? Were the slaves brought from Africa to work the farms? Now, let me see here, this so-called free-market system has a new non-union twist to it—no physical chain this time. That's a positive step! Next stage.

Dollars are OK, too, but we all need to be loyal to a higher truth.

Yes, there are many discourses on government's ineffectiveness, here, but there is that certain amount of progress and spiritual contentment that cannot be denied. Many of the discontented people are not even taxpayers and have never voted. The tendency to believe that government should give them all things free is rampant here. One has to realize that "freedom" doesn't means "freeness." Mankin is not trying to trivialize this point, but this freeness-mentality seems to be a universal thing. An example of the freeness-approach is the inebriated migrant who read the "**Free Tibet!**" slogan on a car. She immediately asked for her free Tibet. The driver was jubilant in agreement that Tibet should be free; he completely misunderstood that she wanted her free Tibet as advertised. Imagine, not knowing what Tibet is, but being willing to accept it as long as it is free! Some things have to be made free of course, but respect is generally earned.

Things have changed on this island, and the people must realize they are dealing with a country that is trying to stay afloat. There is no more Colonial Development &Welfare (CD&W) funds to give them handouts as the rulers from the past Empire usually did. Even that did not help us too much. Remember! You wanted independence, you wanted to be mature, but you are unwilling to bear the costs. You still wanted to be a child, on someone else's farm—an absentee farm? Sounds a little like slavery. We all know the rulers are lethargic sometimes; OK, many times. A case in point, where people donate gifts (books, medical supplies, etc.) to the island, and there are problems getting government clearance. Are these gifts not given release certificates because there is something wrong with them, Mr. Minister? How about your making arrangements with others; your returning nationals to work at home then reneging on your promises on the prices of "returning statuses" in the clearing of their belongings through customs? Are you still doing that, or are you now more streamlined? Well, we all have to go through changes, and changes can be traumatic!

Hear is another change. The Rastafarians decided to enter politics. A Rastafarian political party is long overdue because as a group, they raised our consciousness about pride in being of a different hue from the ruling group. Sometimes they were "far out" from the consensus mainstream ideas, but they never wavered in their approach in denouncing the "*downpressors*" (even those in their midst like the unconscionable wishy-washy political church leaders who proliferated the Caribbean church scenes). They hammered home the concept of Black self-respect like a pestle beating (husking) rice in a mortar. They refused to bow and give into the popular creed of European skin-supremacy when others had long given up the fight under economic duress and physical torture from a docile and mostly uncaring population. They would not be denied. They may not have all gone to their African homeland as was their original wishes (or concept), but they found an international home—possibly going much further than Howell and the other zealots would have even dared to imagine in the earlier years. Profound respect and admiration is due to these Rastafarians who bore the brunt of ridicule and brutality while preaching respect **for the** disadvantaged people of the darker hue. Those were the days, when the British ruled supreme. In those days most Rastas identify with the Israelites. (Is it the Judaeo-Christian concept that they believe that they were mass transported to Babylon—Western World—from Africa?) This identification with Israel of the Christian Bible caused them to see the Arabs as despicable slave traders. To most Rastas, and Caribbean Blacks at that time, the Moslem indoctrination was considered inimical to Black progress—a foreign religion that still trades in Black slaves. One young Rastafarian once asked if Christianity was a non-foreign religion that breeds slaves. One has to remember that was long before the recent discussion about the 1990s slavery of the Black Southern Sudan Christians by the Moslem Arabs of Northern Sudan. Now, there is a radical shift within the Rastafarian Movement to embrace Moslem ideas. The feeling is that Western Christianity is too worldly to lead them on the "Inner Path." It should be remembered that true Rastas had always questioned the beliefs and icons of Christianity, which refused to show any of their hierarchy as being Black. A mystical Rastafarian once vehemently argued this point with a dogmatic Christian evangelist. He told the inflexible preacher that they each may be heading for the same spiritual point, "...but how can you expect me to genuflect before some unfavorable graven images while needlessly counting some of the I multi-colored beads while trying to make the conceptual become actual, this day? Wait!" A very good point; how can you choose to follow the Spiritual agenda of a 'white icon' which causes you pain? A salient point that numerous Caribbean preachers had no wish to hear, because the people had discovered the truth. It possibly reminded them too much of the truthfulness of Jesus the Christ!

Mankin reminds himself of the ways of the original Rastas. He recalls the first real conversation other than the outlandish, and then threatening, call of, "FIRE fi you!" — meaning burn all the oppressors. It should be noted that this statement was not color conscious, seeing that the Britons had predominantly black faces wielding the sticks and guns. (Why not, give the orders, and let them keep the brutality "all in the family"?) A little different from the North American way, eh? Ah, but similar results!

The discussion was between a bearded Asiatic Indian name Ras Raj Hindustan I and a radical Rasta who everyone knew as Jah Rastafari The-Living-I. They were smoking beside the river while debating the laws of Jah. Scene! Raj believed that Indians were the original Dreads from Northern India. The Living-I took a draw from his chillum pipe before giving it to his Indian compatriot. "Take Dread I," said the Rastaman. "You agree then," said Ras Raj, citing that Indians came to the island from about 1845 to 1910. "You knew nothing about locks before we come here in 1845. The African descendants did not even know about Cali in them days, I." "You mean Kali, I" "No, Dread I. The Indo man means Cali, the weed marijuana, or ganja." "So Ras Hindustan I One, what the I telling this I…that the Hindus were even the first Nazarene this day?" "No High Up, the mortal One, can't even take them credit this day, I." "But Ras Raj, the I, sees a picture of the Africans with locks, so how come the I now uttering that this I ancestors lack the know-l*edge* of locks?"

"Movement of mankind from place to place bringeth know-*ledge* everywhere, Jah Rasta."

"I and I says Pow**as** to move-**mants** Hindustan I, I hath **over**stand thy sounds."

"Hail, Up Jah! Pow**as** to sounds and move-mants…there can be no fear in the I and I structure this day," sleepily muttered Ras Raj as he reached for the sweltering herbal pipe.

"Beat down Babylon fear I…yes, lightening strike, thunder clap, and the weak hearts quake. R-A-S-T-A FAR-I LIVES!"

Mankin remembered the sleepiness of the village on the gurgling riverbanks. He also knew that the term Dreadlocks is considered originating from a specific island. The original root possibly means, "you are looking dreadful," possibly *unkempt* in a non-European way. You have gone the ways of the primitive African. "The boy look dreadful!" Anyway, the new idea, now, is that the meaning is a fear of God. **Is that so?**

Out of the Rastafarian movement comes many changes; even Ska the grass-roots music—the "motion of the people." This was one of the forerunners of the reggae beat, which has now turned into some type of newly found church music in the USA. Is this a transmigration of spiritual energy, where the secular group tries it first then it migrates to the spiritual group? Or, is there money to be made here? Just questioning the Ska transition. Perhaps those on the island are not aware that the music is still around! Well?

Now, we hear that the powerful **Regg-ae music is considered a** contributing factor for the young errant behaviors? Some Overseas parents consider it as contributing to the degeneration of the family, with its crime and dance hall shootouts. Other groups use the music for capital gains, but disassociate themselves completely from the Caribbean immigrants when the music stops playing; kicking them back into reality without some usual, and expected, monetary kickbacks. Why blame them? We seem to be very excellent at destroying each other. Who wants to be involved in mayhem, police harassment, and murder? The control of the overseas Caribbean festivals completely passed to the hands of **"others"** who can see only cash in this adventure. The feeblemindedness and the silly divisive group mentality of the Caribbean islanders allowed others to displaced them as the organizers and financial beneficiaries of a wonderful arrangement (entertainment). They are just contented to take the "center stage" in this entertainment, while the profits go to people with brains. Perhaps the guys are just playing for the "pure entertainment of the guys on the balcony," and cash is not a factor. The "balcony group" owns him, you say. Oh, I see…but has anyone recently told him he should wake up, because this is not pre-1838 when William Wilberforce was alive! Has anyone here remembered some talk about, "raise without pay"? You said it! Yes, but Mankin knew he was not "blazing any fire," but to give away our resources so carelessly will put us in trouble. Such an action will not just marginalize us but could place us in the dumps where we may fight even the Mr. John's Crows for sustenance. Do you actually want to be looking up into the sky while competing with the vultures exclaiming that they "come from sky to come rob I" —a type of Crow-bait dialogue if you understand—or is it *over*stated?

What happens here is that we as a group misinterpreted the 1990s free-market strategy as freely made available to others. Remember, sometimes the play of life is not made for us to physically dance but to listen and understand.

The systematic commercialism of reggae and publicity of the Rastafarian lifestyle created an economic boom for the nation. It means the superimposition of values that were once (and are still) considered inimical to Western civilized way of life. It is ironic to see the commercialism of international artists who fought against the "Babylonian system," being presently idolized by those who were the main oppressors in the struggle for freedom and equality. The commercial boys from Uptown see money, no, not a quick buck, but millions! It is not funny when one remembers the types whom usually decried Ska, Rock Steady, and Reggae as a "down there" fun for those people. Has anyone remembered the Ska craze when a certain band decided that it was the originator of Ska? It had a dancer who decided to export it to the good old USA. Of course, the real dancers were not invited; they were not of the "moneyed, business class," Uptown *locally white* and blue-eyed types. Can't have them; these guys have the wrong hue and may want to ask for the wrong type of food! Can't have these people making the mistake of asking for "salt fish" as that other guy did at the hotel in Haiti—remember that incident? Anyway, what is so wrong with a craving for roasted breadfruit, especially if the man wanted to maintain his weight for professional reasons! Does anyone ever consider that the man spoke no French, and the menu was in that language; therefore, he might have seen nothing on the menu he understood. Well, we all have to eat, anyway, but asking for that type of meal is really taking a joke too far from home. He was far from his kitchen, anyway. Sir, next time, for posterity sake, please exhibit a modicum of decorum. Now, we can all beat up the man, but we were not in the man's place. Well, we all know who introduced breadfruit to the man's island and for which reason, too. If any foreign-born island-wanna-bes—children of island parentage—do not know why, do not be ashamed. This knowledge will not put a *blight* on your **bountiful** career. No need to cause a social mutiny. You may still enjoy some life in Tahiti! Riddle me this, and riddle me that.

It seems truthful that economics is "the engine of deceit." The previous Rastas lifestyle was the preaching of political gospel against the stifling British "ole boy system." During those days, the timid populace, who referred to them as "ole dutty rastas" while toadying to identify with the stifling (but orderly) European spirit, generally abandoned the Rastas. Nothing was wrong with that, either; march to your own drums. But, what has drastically changed in the last generation, except the departure of the Colonial master? Now, the Rastafarian ideology and the reggae music are the rescuers of a thriving economic boom in the wake of Bob Marley's prominence. **The middle class and the commercial groups** that oppressed Garvey are still there with their same racial ideas. Now, they sell Rastafarian memorabilia to keep their businesses afloat. No negative mention is now made of the "dutty rastas;" that would not make dollars and "sense." Do you think we should name them, and then remind them of their history of brutality towards the local people? Remind them of their brutality in bashing the heads of innocent people at Pinnacle. In those time when the local inhabitants showed no human interest, they were all too engrossed in playing the illegal urban Chinese number racket of *drop pan* and *peaka peow*. The latter gambling game they did not even understand. It was a time when mothers cut their sons' hair to the scalp, alluding they wanted to become "dirty rastas." It was a time when only pejorative terms were used in describing all non-European experiences, especially when referring to anything with an African identity.

Some people believe in nothing and practice everything to get an economic edge. They believe in the tactical adage, "say many things, practice everything, but agree to nothing." Yes, Mankin understands the practicality— "dem belly full but we hungry…a hungry man is an angry man," telling us that our crippling needs will dictate our politics. But, we still have to stand up for something important, like our rights and our self-respect. One wonders what H. Archibald **Dunkley, Joseph Hibbert,** and Leonard **Howell,** the co-founders of the Rastafarian movement, would say if they could now see this island's economic engine, the spin-offs from Rastafarianism and its big-business offshoot, the fashionable Dreadlocks. The late Ras Ta Fari certainly did not ride his, then, imaginary horse to take them home after his coronation in the 1930s. Not even when he visited them by train as Haile Selassie I in **1966.** In reflection, Mankin still replays Selassie's memorable 1966 visit. This includes the disruption of the honor guard at the airport. The British BBC told the world about that one. The BBC announcements sounded as if such disruptions could not have happened if the British were still the rulers on the island. They may have been correct about that. Credit is due to their ability to organize things; they are truly very competent administrators. Then there was the mistaken airport interview of a certain lady who was not directly connected to the Emperor's entourage. That was another embarrassment. But the most memorable experience was Mankin getting up close to see Selassie one-to-one at the rural train station. Mankin remembered the place was packed with people, waiting to get the best location. All the better areas were taken, so Mankin decided to see the Emperor when he passed. The train came and the Emperor's coached stopped directly in front of Mankin, as if it was planned. The esteem guest calmly stood up, made eye contact, smiled, and respectfully bowed his head. Mankin did likewise. They just stood there looking at each other, as a quiet smile played on the Emperor's face, before the anxious and stampeding onlookers realized they were at the wrong coach! To this day Mankin still questions why no audible information was passed between them. An opportunity missed.

Irrespective of what happened prior to, during, or after Selassie's visit, the Rastafarian movement has left a lasting international impression. It has unfortunately given a certain island the international recognition as a group of trouble making, super radicals who are always roaming the Earth, preaching "down with the inhumane ruling power structure." Recently, the new international agenda for this island seems to come more from a crime perspective. Anyway, one has to take the thick with the thin. Perhaps we need to give a special thanks to Howell, who frightened British monarch George V's servants on the island so much that they sent him to prison for two years on a trumped-up treason charge. Imagine the logical British power structure believing that the Blacks on this small island were going to smoke some ganja, beat their drums, and then pay homage to an African, Ethiopian Emperor Haile Selassie instead of the British king. The orderly British were notorious for sending Rastafarians to prison. They hated the people with a passion. Mankin remembered, with a period of clarity, the utterance of the defiant (or is it well-centered) Ras Steplight when he "powered down" one of those cruel and unjust judges, "before the world was I, where were you? If you open your eyes, you will eventually know us you son of Jezebel." Anyway, let's not forget that Jezebel was a Queen with an almost exclusionary name. Famous or notorious depends on whose religion you surrender to.

"Hail up Jah Ras Steplight!" a man of vision from the misty time.

The man Bob Marley at one of his last concerts in Santa Cruz, California, made statements in his salutations that were then and even now considered very controversial outside mainstream Western society. He looked around the audience, which incidentally had only a few Blacks (yes, possibly less than ten), and then said his prayer. In those days, reggae was not as appealing to American Blacks. It was too primitive, too unpretentious, with its in-your-face racial political overtones—definitely not enough glitz. Its appeals were only to white intellectuals and the politically astute. A great irony. Astute? Perhaps Mankin should rethink the word *astute*, because in the audience was a doctoral candidate from Berkley whose thesis was on the Rastafarians. Now, where would you go to learn about the authentic Rastas? Where? No, not specifically a place called Trench Town on a certain island. We should not get into the naïve mindset of most North American and Briton youths that people in the "***Trench***" just walked around in a heady haze with carrot-size "spliffs" dangling from their mouths. They have laws against that there, too. Anyway, there is one thing we know; it is inconceivable that a scholar would go to Santo Domingo to learn about Rastafarinism! This scholar was so impressed that Mr. Marley could elevate himself from a depressed neighborhood as Trench Town to be an international messenger of conscience. Really, Ms. Scholar, but you had never been to Trench Town, so what standard were you using? Perhaps a more socially advantageous neighborhood of Santo Domingo where the "color scheme" is less threatening to you? Perhaps the Berkley One has truly gone berserk-ly! Some tribute is due to the Berkley One for stepping out beyond her unruffled horizon in search of knowledge. Anyway, it is the similar scholarly misconception that caused foreign reggae music lovers to say "2 rasses" instead of *to rass*. There is so much misunderstanding of that dialect. The generally advertised, sick and annoying, utterance of "Yeah, Mon" is now well used. But, the most pitiful saying was when Mankin realized foreigners made the mistake of quantifying the word *rass*, and using it as a greeting, too. What happens when three or more gather? How many rasses are there now? This is indeed a computerized world; they really like numerics here! Yes, we all know the Western culture tries to quantify everything, but saying "2-rasses, mon!" One thought the saying was "to rass." What will these foreigners come up with next, $2+n^{th}$ rasses? The more the better, eh? What about taxes! What is a "rass," anyway? Now, don't get into the psychological mindset that using it soothes your behavior and keeps you from committing a felony.

At that concert, Marley repeated himself about his belief in Haile Selassie and the final overthrow of the oppressive Babylonian system. He ended with the clincher, "with apology to none!" Rhythm music— "dem belly full, but we hungry…a hungry man is an angry man!" A statement of freedom that rings the knell of the numerous apologist "quashies" that seem to dominate the migrant leadership groups. Perhaps they have too much imaginary butter on their bread, as one dear fellow from jolly ole England (the Black imperialistic type) relayed to Mankin while walking along Bathurst Street in Toronto, Canada. Imagine refusing to visit your homeland, because you cannot heap a quantity of butter on your bread. The man should know by now that "man shall not live by bread alone." Yes, yes, we knew the butter on it makes it not "bread alone," but let's not trivialize the point here! Mankin marveled how so many immigrants can praise their country but never make a conscientious effort to retire there. Instead, they encourage others to go as tourists. The contrary principle here is that people from all over the world travel to your homeland, like it, and make preparations to live there. They then finally retire there in the sunshine, turning the place into an upscale Mecca for international, absentee summer retirees. When the immigrant tries to return, the real estate price is out of sight, and he is out of luck, because he has lost his connection while preaching (or seeking) abundance in a strange "seasonal" land. Even foreigners, who Mankin heard in the past referring to Rastafarians as "a kooky cult called Rastafarian," were observed in Negril dancing to the reggae beat. Apparently, what was kooky yesterday has you cooking today. Justice is finally done!

Now, we hear the new trend in justice on the Islands is to torture by flogging. Note that the gunmen are not flogged, only others who don't use guns. Why? Is it because gunmen are willing to kill, whereas others are simply malcontents, trapped on an island without opportunities. What happens if these simple ones migrate to the next threatening level: the dreaded gunman? It should be remembered that the British could use this type of torture effectively because they kept guns out of the hands of the populace. And, they are masters at hiding their misdeeds; also, their friends have similar intentions and power. The new island rulers have no such clout. The new rulers made the mistake of clandestinely introducing ballistic weapons in their countries, while trying to maintain power. Unfortunately for us all, after the gunman's work was accomplished, he refused to relinquish his power, similar to his mentors, the **poli*tricksians.*** Has anyone here remembered the story about the mongoose and the snake. It is, hereby, emphatically denied that comparing either the politics-person or his associates, the gunmen, as either a snake or as a mongoose. They are all human beings who have selected a path in life; at least we all hope they are human. It would be nice if neither exercised their options, but that is just a wish, now. The deed is already being done. Alas! Now, we hear of the emergence of new, high-technology robotic torturing devices, introduced by the politicians (sons of slaves), to cripple the new generation of their brothers—the lower class criminals. Perhaps they believed it worked for their past Colonial (slave) masters, so it must work for them, too. Yes, the usage of old and ineffective solutions for today's problems. The old slavers usually used people of the similar race to inflict pain on each others ("Let them keep it in the family ole boy,") but the "New Faces" found a new device in the high-tech field to do their bidding (or, is it whipping?) The mindset among the "New Group" must be if they don't practice birth control, then kill them after birth with the gun or by torture in prison! Of course, it is only the poor, generally people of one type of complexion and race, that is being tortured as always. This time there is a difference though; they are being tortured by their own people. Granted, the criminals committed crimes generally on their own racial groups, although not exclusively. An equal-opportunity group, they are, with the same consistency—theft, rape, and or brutal death.

Ever wonder how come these types of tortures are not considered for the European and North American societies? What are the differences between these societies and those who recently, secretly planned crippling its citizen while they are incarcerated? What is the main difference with these inhabitants except economics and location? As Mankin contemplated these thoughts, he wondered how comfortable he would be with a doctor who supervised these tragedies. Is the detestable concentration camp physician, Dr. Mengele, still alive? If not, then who are present at these torturing sessions? No doctor is present, you said? I know a healer could not be present, but then even healers crave pieces of silver—blood money tainted with agony. Yes, we all heard that Judas Iscariot later repented, but the painful deed had already been done. Now, would you trust any person who enjoyed or supervised torturing another human? How would you feel about putting a very sharp knife into such a person's hand while you lay naked and unconscious on a table? Would you feel comfortable while such a person attempted cutting into your flesh, performing an operation, or delivering your baby? Do you understand how easy it would be for such a callous person to commit murder? "Oops. Nurse, cover it up; this operation was unsuccessful. Oh well, want a beer later?" Think about that; your loved ones are outside awaiting your recovery from **Dr. Death's** operation, possibly even saying their many "Our Fathers," asking for Divine help. Then they are told, "Sorry this time Death won, again!" This is serious, so don't expect hearing some TV sinister, villain-like, evil triumphant laughter to end this stanza. The new status now will be—a patient nearly recovers! The new statistics— Death wins, Life lost, Game over...

Numerous migrants believe other's problems are not theirs when the media plays to the populace before sentencing migrants from another island. There is always an outcry whenever someone from another group other than the usual institutional target group is targeted with injustice. Who do the newly targeted group generally run to first? The group that is generally the "whipping boy" of the system. The other groups are always looking for solidarity, shouting, **"They discriminated against** us!" Where are they when the innocent "others" are targeted? Possibly hiding under their fragile, "physically unlike them" veneer of make believe social acceptance. "We are not like those people...they deserve to be treated so...always making trouble while listening to that noisy reggae music. Don't you always see on TV how the police handle them?" Really? How did they handle you in your innocence? Now, you want help, and "there is no one around to help!" Mankin watched many unaware migrants sneering and jeering the noble men in the **Million Man March**, contemptuously asking why are they marching. "Can't you see?" You believe they have no commitment to anything, eh? You should just hope your time to find out never comes! All African ancestry should have realized by now that the most well-organized Black group in the world is in the United States of America. All the others are just mere pretenders. South Africa would bear honorable mention, but what do these two groups have in common except the Black population? No, not just the most people in prison.

Recently we hear that many of the migrant guys in **Overseas Prisons** are asking for correspondences to keep in touch with people from their own country, because their own culture has finally given up on them and their criminal habits. Even the government of their native land is also unwilling to communicate with them, saying they mostly committed wrongs against their own people Overseas. Now, the question arises, "What would have happened if their crime had been against others?" A little tricky, here now, isn't it Mr. Politician? Some older migrant groups may still remember other original gun users like Ivanhoe 'Rhygin' Martin, who was one of the first notorious gunmen. (No, Bogus Boy does not count. He was part of the dissatisfied System, although his case has some merit, too. But then, we all have some points to make, good or bad!). The difference between these two gun wielders is that the "Rhygin One" was not part of the System so—you guessed it—he was killed. And, **the** "Bogus One," being a part of the System, had a good lawyer and was spared to live imprisoned, labeled as a madman. Yes, he was **not "speared"** with bullets! It would appear that people who choose to join the habitual criminal fraternity should know the system in which they operate. Apparently, the simplistic migrant wrongdoers are not observing this rule. While they prey on their communities, they are in turn being preyed on by incompetent lawyers. As one of their types remarked recently, "Service with a sentence!" It should be noticed here that the legal incompetence of their defenders are not color dependent. The legal field is level with an equal opportunity for incompetence in all groups. Unfortunately, it affects the migrant the most because of their quantity of social carelessness and unwillingness to learn something worthwhile—like understanding the challenges of a complex world.

ISLAND OPPORTUNITIES

The Powers on the islands act as if they don't realize that people can be effectively trained in school. Not enough schools are being built here to accommodate the young. Because of this scarcity, some principals in the high schools act as little demi-gods. **An educator in one of the more prominent high schools once told a brilliant** Overseas-returning student (after giving him an entry test which he easily passed) that he would not accept him because the student would not obey him, seeing as how he was from a foreign country. Now, tell me how a man can put obstacles in the way of young ones, and considered himself a pillar of society, an educator, no less! Perhaps, it would be better for society if his type had been in the way of the falling pillars during the biblical Samson's destruction of the Philistine's temple. Why take away a dream when you can give a chance to excel? This young one was returning to his birthplace, because he has no legal document to stay Overseas. This small-minded pedagogue felt that his only authority was his cane. He even tried emulating the moldy wigged character, the British principal portrayed in the old commercial "When you eat your Smarties, do you eat the red one last?" Perhaps he ate his "smarts" too early—a principal practicing principles of exclusion with expatriates because he believes he may not be able to easily brutalize another young human. Now, that student grew up and despised his own country with a vengeance. If his hue were different, would the principal have being a little more considerate? The more things seem to change the more they remain the same. Mankin remembered, long ago, a friend being interviewed for a scholarship. The interviewer was very jovial until he realized that the person being interviewed was not the child of his friend down the road. The interviewer's whole attitude changed. Although the student was a deserving person, the interviewer had no intention of continuing the interview. He became surly and abruptly ended the interview. The irony was his friend had no son; so one still wonders how friendly the man was with his friend. Is there a story here? Of course, a brilliant young person was again denied an opportunity to get an education. This is a system where exclusion is the principle of life. The powerful ones only do favors for friends. Their rationale is to exclude all other deserving people, hence mediocrity reigns supreme. Can you please try and give others a chance, Mr. Educator? The "others" who don't join your social circles or political affiliation—help us, please. Have you ever heard the saying, "**a** mind is a terrible thing to waste"? Sir, (or is it little Mr. "Mampala") you have wasted your spirit in denying the needy, deserving ones. Why are you such a coward that you would not take a chance with this young expatriate, seeing that no antisocial behavior was involved? Your country now recruits doctors, don't you?

Here children are being constantly introduced from their infancy to the most wanton, corruptive lyrics by an expansive group of demented singers who console themselves by debasing their mothers (if they have one), wife, sisters, and daughters. The greater tragedy is that the women seem to enjoy being artistically abused in the basest forms. They dance with gusto and take pleasure in the most sexually explicit lyrics, extolling the virtue of men demeaning women—a new trend in female sexuality, perhaps! Mankin ponders what these singers have against women's vaginas! He cannot believed they all came through a "Caesar's section," and even if they did, what do they have against women? Now, even the women are in the act of abusing themselves, exchanging curses that are specifically directed at themselves and other female's sexual organs. Is this not comparable with the old free-market economic slavers? Similar to the children being sold by Black tribes in Africa to the West for a piece of gaudy looking *chickenpox rag*. This led to the crude plantation mentality to exploit even your mother for a price. Why are we not too surprise at this? Females are the mutilators of their own kind. Imagine female babies genitalia being mutilated by grown, and supposedly sane, females. So what is a little ribaldry for money between women... "play de music, jump like *leggo* beasts..." Well, they are the only gender that can bring people here, so they will sing, dance, and butcher whomever they please. Stop the whining; mothers rule!

During adolescence there are little or no available jobs. There are only a few high schools to attend...not many training schools either...exclusion is practiced with a vengeance. Are these contributive to errant young behaviors, Mr. Judge? Why should he care, anyway? He cannot believe that his children will be affected. Yes, those he had with his favorite woman or legal wife. The others can be whipped to within an inch of their lives or even killed—he did not link his name with them anyway. They were possibly an embarrassment after his fun. His social facade would be shattered. Perhaps his "outside" children's mothers lied to him—they were using birth control—so that gave him the excuse to rest his pious little soul that the baby was for someone else. He may be right too, because so many of these societies are sexually speculative! No, not in a mercenary way, but in a linked, associative way with a baby as the key factor for economics gain and control. A woman's way to associate with a man whom she decided can help her. So what is wrong with that; men fight to marry women who can help them, too. The problem here is the woman is generally left with the baby when the fun is over. Many times **she** miscalculated her control. Men have fun, then see responsibility and flee! A better equation for the woman would be to enjoy the ride. Take the money with some honey, too, without having a baby, then exercise her mobility and drop out of circulation, but who can script anybody's life for them? Anyway, judges are human, and reflect the trend in the society, so cruelty and murder is their bag, also. So, do not be surprised about dreadful judges who are trying to whip the populace into a submissive pulp! Just remember, force has an equal and opposite reaction, and the judiciary group has tried brutality before. Boomerang! Remember? But whoever lived long enough to truthfully adjudge these events in this play called life?

Mankin has seen numerous plays and dances on this plane called Earth. He has also observed many disappointments, the heritage of mortality, as the saying goes. He has seen many a Rastafarian strut their stuff to the hypnotic rhythm of the drums (while "putting some smokes" in their lungs, and watching "Little Miss **"Dem de Wi"** dance according to an older matriarch). According to the old revered matriarchs, "Little Miss Dem de Wi" is the phenomenon of the "dancing lady," imaginary or real, seen through the haze of the female ganja trance. Most village smokers claimed the female ganja is the cleaner and the most potent types. Perhaps the clinical British knew something here when they made specific legal prohibition against the female cannabis type. "Can't have the bloody natives dancing without visibly moving—too contrary to known physical principles." Were they thinking that Newton might not be able to explain this esoteric stationary "dancing" principle? Perhaps such unexplained Afro-principle could topple their Empire. Well?

Other dancers have also come to mind. Among them is an internationally renowned Indian dancer whose message was the emancipation of women in her native India. With her, Mankin has this great empathy, because freedom is a spiritual requirement for all mankind (make that people).

"Politically correct you say?" Her dance was a thing of grace in all aspect of the word *movement* and in the aesthetic presentation of her attire. Her performance was quite an experience, but the most memorable ritualistic dance was the dance of the "Blackhat Masters." These monks displayed what it is to move in synchronism with sounds. It was as if they were one with the cymbals and drums. As Mankin watched the Blackhat Ones step and twirl through their dances, he pondered the gravitational field and spherical movement of the planet Earth in its orbit relative to the other heavenly bodies. He thought about the dizzy speed at which the Earth turns while we "claim" to stand on solid ground. He thought about the force of gravity, which holds the planets in their orbits, but yet, is so accommodating that the birds can penetrate it with utmost ease. On the dimly lit stage, the Blackhat Masters do their thing in unison to sound and with each other. Mankin could only watch and observe in his mind's eyes the solemnest of the dancing of the newly "emancipated ones" in 1838 as they reflected on those friends, relatives, and acquaintances who had not lived to see the day of freedom. Their dance was a remembrance of pain and toil, of the inhumane treatments of those who perished under the tortures of whips, brutality, rapes, old age, loss of spirit, and other rigorous forms of despicable punishments devised for their conformity to institutionalized enslavement. Their dance was a remembrance of the losses of those in a watery grave during the notorious "passage" from possibly a free homeland across the oceans to the living hell of the Western fields of purgatory. Could they really dance physically, or let their spirit dance, while feeling the numerous tell-tale body signs of brutality as they looked through teary swollen eyes and remembered friends who long ago vanished into the shadowy worlds of their minds? Mankin could understand them going through their soul-refreshing dance of freedom, dancing to the freedom song: "…you lik me, mi lik you back. Tenke massa."

This was not a song of visual, or physical stimulation but a mandate for freedom and spiritual equality where one is judged as an equal—one-to-one. It was a promise that is yet to be fulfilled over a century after the abolishment of human chattel slavery. Even generations after the late MLK gave his brilliant 1963 speech in the Capitol of the present-day "Big Boys on the Block."

As Mankin alternates his reality by time-traveling between the past and present, he reflects on stories that he heard in his infancy, when all things were considered ideal and simplistic. In his view, we all seem to feel this way whenever we mention younger carefree days. Of course, there are exceptions to these rules. One cannot believe the slaves had it the same way. They were persons like us, so perhaps they did, too. (So let us say a prayer for those who have passed, or pour some of your good libation on Mother Earth in memory to those who struggled to give us a better **understanding**). **In those care-free days,** there was nothing to fear except the childish, imaginary ghosts, which some people even now claim are real! Or, perhaps some feared displeasing of one's parents. Mankin reflected on these things as the Blackhat Masters synchronized their movements to time on a dimly lit stage. Yes, we are one with all things, connected with the same breath of air, with Life itself. We are one. Dance your dance Blackhat Ones. Imagine either Nanny or Cudjoe, the **brilliant Maroon** leaders, watching the people dancing to the freedom songs when they repulsed the British slavers after a hard fight for their freedom. Here again we have to digress and question why are we following the Spaniards, calling this group of freedom-loving people Maroon? Why are we not calling them by the name of their origins, their tribal names, whether it is the Ashanti or some other tribe? Let's call them by their names. We do not call the British, the brutal Belgians or the other oppressive European people "slavers." And, that is what they are. So, why are we still calling these freedom fighters "wild," which is actually a translation from the Spanish word *cimarron*? "Wild," for some, means freedom to be unshackled from a master's wishes, to roam freely. These so-called "Wild People" fought the British to gain their freedom in 1740, many generations before the enslaved "Tame Others" would become free through sympathy. Perhaps these people were really from the Ashanti in Ghana. How can anyone who knows the valuable history of the indomitable **Nana Yaa Asantewaa** (1900), the Ashanti warrior queen who showed the timid patriarchy what true freedom and leadership is all about, mistake this? Again the common enemy of freedom, then, was the deceptive British!

The very thought of overcoming vastly superior, well-equipped forces of darkness to live another day will drive anyone to some form of spiritual ecstasy. Do not just rejoice as the air expands and contracts your lungs but look to the beauty in nature; live for another sunset and feel the warmth on your body. Rejoice to see beauty and respect in the eyes of friends and even enemies, to touch another, and feel the warmth and heartbeat or even synchronize heartbeats in a more personal love. Perhaps you must weep, while looking at the inert and mutilated bodies of your young loved ones, the casualties of freedom, who had quite recently given you so much pleasure with their young innocence. Perhaps you altruistically wish you had died instead, but you know if that had occurred you would probably have condemned them to a fate worst than their early death—slavery! Wouldn't you give thanks for being alive, by observing nature's other beings, stirring with the inherent flow of life—the life energy which uniquely defines us all? Rejoice to know you can walk away without being violently forced to come back. Rejoice to be "wild" with a freedom to choose...even death!

In the ritual dances, one should not forget **Poco Mania, also;** they, too, have a path to play in their **dance,** although it may not be publicly well-defined by some. Or, should we embolden our statement with, "in the background of your minds, it still furiously roams, but your face calmly reflects the acceptable image of Christianity or another socially acceptable mainstream religion." If this were not so, how could there be so many advertisements in your ethnic newspapers from these occultist, Madam X people, promising you clairvoyance and a cure for all your ills, imaginary or real? Are you "rubbing up" with all these types of nauseating, smelling ointments and "turning your rolls" while muttering tongue-twisting (tongue-tying), incoherent mumbo-jumbos after reading some destructive sounding Psalms from the Christian Bible? And, what's with this "Jumping the Mial, and drawing sounds"?

Wait! One has to be very cautious here about this *incoherent mumbo-jumbo* thing, and remember what happened in the Upper Room in Jerusalem during the day of Pentecost. Observers, then, believed the Christian disciples were talking in strange tongues, too. We definitely will not continue this line of *"inguistic"* speculation, by getting into some silly religious discourse about the relationship of the Tower of Babel and past language changes. Perhaps it's better here just to say one doesn't understand the Poco Maniac's communication! Satisfied with this explanation, Ms. Poco Priestess? Ok, then start smiling and stop "cutting your eyes" at us; go on with your jumping around your mysterious *"table."*

Give us some of your sound vibrations too...bam-baba-bam-hmmm. Ahem. Ahem. Ahem... That's better.

And why this usage of "white rum" in all these "affairs" of the spirit world? Who are these guys who are recommending this color rum? Are they part of the marketing conglomerate, getting some kickbacks for their recommendations? Eh, Mankin, has to ask these question because the Wizards, and the "Mothers Xs" are all business people, too. Take the view that they are also a part of the free-market structure. They may not be your usual commercial psychics, but they may make just as much without paying the dreaded system fee—taxes! Perhaps they used their combined occult knowledge to keep the "Caesar's fee-gatherers" away. Anyway, why this special color of alcohol? Are the inhabitants of the spirit world playing exclusionary drinking games on the living? By now, we think they would get politically correct and be more integrated and even ask for darker colored rums, or even light beers. We can't believe all these Obeahists are just dealing with non-integrationist ghosts. Perhaps it's time we picket them for not recommending other color alcohol? This type of exclusionary alcoholic choice can be bad for business; get with the new business trends of the 21st century," Mr. Do-goodman" or move over and let the new, trendy psychics or wrapped head "glass and water" readers take over for the new Millennium.

We all can agree that migrants worshipped many deities, although their claim is always that they believed in one religion, generally Christianity. They always denied that they were seeking a type of "Celestial Insurance," or more Double Assurance, where all religion is encouraged, because they are afraid to leave out any deity who may be able to help them. Their behavior, many times, caused one to suspect their belief and wonder if they might be praying to the wrong ONE... "Oh ye of little faith!" If they are true believers, then why are they paying so much money to their sorceress, wizard, Santeria, priestess, Obeahist, or any other names these mystifying "expeditors" choose to use, just to be told something the migrants quite likely already knew? Are most immigrants superstitious? Yes, we all know they put horseshoes and other things over the entrance to their homes. So what does that prove? The trendy joke is they all buy horseshoes, thereby driving up the price, but none of them owns a horse. They can't even ride. Ever heard about the North American-born trainee Obeahist who placed the horseshoe upside down over the doorway? So you did not know there is a correct way? Well, some people have no spiritual *knowledge*. Anyway, the Trainee One was blamed for concentrating the energy in the wrong direction. Apparently, his newly developed Obeahistic-attunement calculations were off, so he had some focal attenuation in his dream-deciphering matrix. This caused his employer to miss one winning number off his lottery ticket—what a disaster! It seems the trainee was investigating a new quantum principle in horseshoe rotational dynamic energy transfer. The word is out that the Islands' old mainstream Obeahists defrocked him for his deviation from well-defined fundamental principles. They took away his shiny black ring made from the calabash tree, shading his grandfather's grave. Ah well, trendsetters are always at risk. The word is out that this trainee recently changed his name to Obarus (Obeah-or-us?) and is fine tuning his "business" skills in Virginia.

It is quite likely many migrants are superstitious. Now, what about other people who visit psychiatrists? Are they scientific, mad, stupid, neurotic, psychotic—but certainly not superstitious? So, only poor immigrants from the unsophisticated and uneducated groups visits these fringe "readers!" Is it the same syndrome where the rich have ulcers, but the poor have indigestion? The end results seem to be the same type of pain.

Every living creature tries to avoid pain. Is this a command from a Higher Mind?

Quite likely it is, because pain will certainly take one out of their natural game...no doubt about that...pain reminds us all about the limitation of our mortality. Anyway, Mankin remembered his trip with a well-centered friend; the spiritually inclined and charming "Xialist." While in the air, the "Xialist" closed her eyes and voiced her opinion that she was "**grounding**" the plane to keep it safe on its flight. Mankin did not like the term "grounding the plane," because the idea of flight and ground sounds like contrary principles, when you are in fight. Think flight only, and leave grounding out of it. "Grounding" is when you are not in flight. It is for when you are stationary on the runaway. Think positive thoughts the next time you fly. It impacted Mankin's mind a bit when the "Xialist" got into the concentrated inner-connection of her 'grounding' prayer or wherever she spiritually went. Apparently, it worked, for the flight landed safely and there was great jubilation as the great "concentrator" refreshed herself. Let it be understood here that Mankin is not about to trivialize any of this, because he had no operable wings during that flight. If the spiritual Xialist said she helped the plane to land safely, so be it! Go ahead, Ms. Xialist, do your thing. Laugh if you wish, but remember this; Mankin heard no one frantically screaming "may-day" during that flight. Thanks Xialist. Every migrant group believes that all people have their spiritual connections to hidden powers. Or, at least we believed so! If we all believed so, then could we all be wrong? No need to answer that we may get a surprise.

Here Mankin remembered the story of a group of Spiritualists (no, Occultists is more appropriate). Now, why do you have to make assumptions and think about them as necromancers? Did you know them, or use their services?

These "occultists" were always in opposition because of economic competition and prestige. (What other types of competitions are there anyway? Sex?) Mankin, in his early days, remembered people talking in hushed, apprehensive voices about two warlocks **named "Doubt-all" and "Psyche"** who were supposed to be neighbors, living in some inaccessible place called Smoke Hole. They were not practicing Spiritualists or Goddesses; they were in the clandestine art and practiced clairvoyance and cure—with vengeance for a fee, of course. In his childish mind, then, he always pictured mounds of earth, similar now to pictures of a brownish desolate lunar landscape with smoke lazily spiraling from the top of each mound. His older boyish friends, then, mentioned how these warlocks had mysterious skeletons living with them. It was years later when Mankin realized that none his friends had ever seen a warlock or a skeleton. Now, here he is remembering old tales as he looked at the portrait of a cycling skeleton, mounted in artistic display. Now, he no longer wonders what a mysterious skeleton is. He, now, tries putting this enigmatic skeletal display in his perspective by thinking: ...the skeleton sheds its skin as it pedals along the road from mortality to eternity (not oblivion). It wears no mask, because it sees no threat to its very existence (being), because it is not of this (our) world. The skeleton viewed the living with laughter (amusement) as we cope with changes (chagrin) in our coincidental (hit and miss) world (universe.) While Mankin amuses himself in the disguise of an artiste, time continues with that inner voice informing us that we all have to participate in the ritual dance of the living. Try to resist if you will, but you will always obey the prime command of nature. To do what? To do whatever your belief structure dictates is your choice.

Mankin observed that we all dance for some type of connections, don't we, or are we trying to avoid disconnection? Which one do you think? Yes, you! If not, why did you move to the ghettoes when you could have lived in other places, like Uptown for example, with less stress? You felt a strong connection to the skin color of your compatriots, although you could not stand their behaviors…too loud at times, eh…but you felt more comfortable around them…safety in numbers like a shoal of fishes, seeking safety in a circular whirlpool formation to avoid the roaming predators. Just be warned, our biped predators are everywhere, especially so in your chosen neighborhood!

Perhaps the only true connectedness is the mind-body connection where we feel in harmony within our environment and ourselves. We are our mind, which encapsulates events and replays them back over time for our positive reinforcement or as a corrective force to maintain our perspective. A kind of negative feedback control to maintain our human linearity. We are aware that rituals and totemic references play a large part in the human experience. All culture seems to have their own interpretation of some spiritual accompaniment or a need to avoid certain phenomena or bad vibes! Although all cultures seem to feel they are intertwined with nature, this view is not really pronounced in the Western world. Western culture views the environment as the enemy of human comfort and progress. It should be observed that this belief is not a cultural belief of all highly industrial countries, because the Asiatic industrial giants are keen believers that they are part of nature, and therefore have a natural mindset to honor nature, especially so in their own countries. The Western culture sees humans in confrontation with nature. Who is right, and who is wrong is not the point, there seem to exists a need in all cultures for spiritual connection.

Mankin watched, with curiosity, as the dancers and drummers moved around the campfire in the drumming circle. He wondered why certain cultures seemed to prefer drums and rattles, while others seemed to prefer wind and string instruments. While watching the drummers, he saw the changes in the participants' behaviors as the crescendo of the drums changed tempo. Big Thunder Deer put his palms on the rug and stared in the distance, as if in a trance. He stiffened his back, then slowly stroked the rug with a circular motion as if to say, "You are an entity that had lived before. You deserve respect, now, even in death. Thank you, Mother Earth, for making us very comfortable at this time."

Mankin can understand the totemic significance of the word, *bear* in this man's name. It signifies harmony of being attuned to the Earth's frequencies. One would need this attunement to live through the winter, during the bear's hibernation period. Big Thunder Bear then said a prayer of acknowledgment to Father Sky, Mother Earth, and the Wind that sustained us. Could it be that Big Thunder Bear is in tune with the Spiritual Triad?

Looking at Sleek Running Elk, Mankin wondered if her commitment to a spiritual search was in accordance with the Native American's standard of earthly attuned spirituality or if it was a trendy routine or economically motivated fad. What's new about this? Perhaps nothing in the context of human behavior. We all have our crosses (crescent; inverted, superimposed triangles; yin-yang symbols; or whatever) to bear, even the showy Sleek Running Elk has to play her part, too. As the drummers and dancers seek spiritual solace from a world gone mad with "quickie fixes" and nerdy experts who are always jargonizing us with their intellectual "double speak," Mankin pondered the question, "To what degree can we exercise our freedom of worship in most society? Perhaps we should be asking at this time, "What is our true belief? Is it money or religion (including animism) or is it just anything as long as it pays the bills? What is important in your life? Yes, I mean the overriding concerns—bills or work? Did Mankin leave out something more profoundly enjoyable (to you), here? Bear in mind that sex is not seriously considered under the omitted selection, because it could be considered as either bills or work. You may not choose to answer, here, right now, but Mankin believes there will come a time when all living beings must truthfully give a reply. A time when the "shackles of immobility" hold your legs and finally request a response.

Mankin is aware that the artist allows us to externalize our inner feelings and get in touch with our true selves, away from the *trendiness* of the ever-physical commercial world where the techno-elites use machines to rule the masses. Now, they, too, are gradually forgetting that they are humans. Recently, we became so machine-dependent that the machines finally became our masters. The simple idea of taking a musical instrument to a secluded area and enjoying the music is almost like treason. Can you imagine taking a drum on the edge of any town, away from the city, teeming millions and beginning to play? (So you do not like drums? Then take your violin with you. Elitists! When the revolution comes, we will have to take away your wind.)

Just envision an area where no one would be disturbed, or trespassing would not be a problem. (You don't believe there is such a place in the industrial countries? Keep looking; there is.) One knows the law enforcement people with their other institutional "multi-listening" buddies will show up with a question— "What are you doing here?"

You respond, "Playing my drum."

(If you have a violin, quite likely you will be left alone. They may even return with coffee for you. A drum is just too radical. You are gone; with him (or her), of course.)

"Do you have any id?"

"For my drum!"

Sounds like South Africa! (Or, any other 'free' countries?")

"No, to verify who you said you are."

"I did not say who I am, but here are the papers."

The institution runs your check, and find nothing illegal, but it has to flex its "force." Ever think that the drum beat symbolizes freedom and possibly war? Ask the North American native people about this point. Well, ask any ethnic people. Think it symbolizes a challenge to people in authority? "...come to the gathering of the free spirited ones, and listen, keenly, how you, too, can be truly happy...and possibly pay no taxes... **(What? Don't be silly!)**" Again be careful who is playing the drums; sometimes the System, itself, may fake a "gathering" then all hell will break loose, later...just remember entrapment is a System's project.

"Why don't you come with me?" Ever think of responding to this question in the negative? They finally take you to a psychiatrist or psychologist...for your benefit of course. Ever try to find out which one of these "psych-types" have the suffix "-trist" or "-gist?" Anyway, the "psych-x" person is possibly some intelligent-looking, straight-nosed, smiling, glasses-wearing guy dressed in a white smock. "Psych-x" then looks at you and espouses some of his neat psycho-babble theory: "...you are reliving the security of your missed infancy in your mother's womb when the sounds of her heartbeats were comforting to your development. This type of childhood retrogression is comparable to your beating your little 'tom-tom' to relive the comfort of your infancy..."

Tom-tom? Shades of Tarzan and the Apes!

Bear in mind, here, that the size of the drum would not possibly have bearing on the learned ones' diagnosis, but humor him because he has the power to warehouse you forever, because you dare to be different. He scribbles some hieroglyphic on a paper, telling the authorities to release you, because you are as harmless as tits on a boar hog! Perhaps he reasoned that the drums did not help your fore-parents in Africa (or wherever), so how is it going to help you, now, when there are so many high-tech listening devices and weapons aimed at your head?

This brings up the Orweillian ramifications, which the immigrant has to contend with in these industrialized countries. It seems that people are always being watched by the proverbial "Big Brother" who is always coming up with complex rules to restrict people's freedom in the name of "fighting crime," or the other "biggie" —threat to national security. Here, people are always being numbered against their will and being asked to pay for some long number that you cannot ever commit to memory. Ever try giving your name to a clerk for any type of simple transaction, and being told: "There is a number on your document. Read it to me, please." Have you ever mentally screamed, "No, damn it! Read it your blasted self!" Now, you are not a human being anymore. You actually needed a **netid** to talk with, she and her know-it-all friend in the box, the computer. How can one define this? She is the one with the "blinking box," but you, as an individual, are undefined until her "boxed-in friend" agrees you are alive. Definitely not good! Sigh. You started reading, but you cannot see the friggin' fine print anymore; your eyesight is going, thanks to years of industrial stress and the aging process. How you longed to "throw down" all this complication and just walk away in peace. Yes, "throw down iron," as the Old Villagers usually said. Mankin wondered if anyone here misunderstood the symbolism of the words? Anyway, you read on, speculating your time will come to rest your weary back as others before you seem to do. But wait! Is there some prediction that the social security fund will run out? Now, you have a headache just thinking about that.

Truly, information is the backbone of power, and therefore, commerce (wealth and knowledge), but has there ever been so much abuse of this privilege in the annals of human history? Mankin wondered, in Biblical times, why was it contrary to Divine wishes to number the people…perhaps it was Devil arithmetic to be beaten with a numbering stick. Most immigrants felt like this type of computerized intrusion has destroyed their individuality (humanity, if you will) and treated their very existence as goods in a warehouse to be sold and replenished at the owner's will. To be considered successful the migrants have to be re-schooled (or is it re-tooled) to learn how the **original power group** lives. If you were even "schooled" among them, your background may influence your social mobility. Actually, schooling is considered an ideal locale, where power is discussed from a different level. To understand the original power group is to work with them. This is where the big boys roam; the true battle of Armageddon is fought here. Beware, this is the final move, which determines your very existence after birth!

SCENARIO:

Many times the immigrants tried hard to understand the everyday power language (jargons) used by the power brokers. To get ahead in these industrial societies one must know these scripts, the language tool of the power brokers, because no amount of formal education from any university is going to help you "speak" the languages.

Mankin reflected on an immigrant who went on a training mission to a place called the Silicon Valley, in California—a technological crucible where strange terms like *nerds*, *geeks*, and *techno-gurus* are used to describe brilliant people who one day may own your company. She was introduced to people of diverse cultures in various levels of the corporate structure, who all praised the corporation for its humane treatment of its employees. There was a common language-base for everyone, but each group has its own complex "group speak." With all these strange surroundings, the immigrant decided to bide her time and watch the "runnings" (let events unfold), as the old saying goes.

Mankin understands the paradox of working in these strange environments where the immigrant is very happy to be employed but at the same time feels socially alienated and sad because of the absence of human warmth (a lack of a nourishing environment) where one feels one's contribution makes a difference.

Sometimes the scientists would go one-on-one with the engineers, or with each other, and coin a whole different language for themselves. The great mystery about it was that these strange fellows enjoyed their discussions. They seem to have an affinity for each other's "techno-speak" whereas the other power groups—marketing (the business ivory-towered ones) and the legal group (the whereas-whereas boys) —are always asking the question, "What do you mean by this line?" Of course no one ever understands lawyers, but not being able to understand the other groups was never quite accepted by anyone else. Sometimes, in these meetings, one wonders how anything can ever get accomplished when the language tool is so diversified. The three main groups believe everyone else is out of it. The immigrant referred to the experience as "a little slice of the Tower of Babel"

The key word, here, seems to be *absolutely*, uttered whenever a conversation or explanation is given.

"So, Rick, you think this will fly?"
"Absolutely! It's a go."

Take note, here; never absolutely believe Rick or anyone else until you see the paperwork, and even then beware! Remember, there are no absolutes here. Jingoism and spin-doctors harangue are on the loose, here. They are very, very good, here.

The immigrant went to an inter-departmental meeting to hear the message from on high. Everybody there was so laid back (or at least pretended to be). There were the usual rumors flying around about promotions and lay-offs. She was introduced as the expert from that wonderful world of sunshine and happiness where everything was supposed to be ideal. No one said anything about economic severity from her region. The introduction started with smiles of acknowledgment and extended arms. The group resembled a miniature United Nations, with the names to match. Everyone had a special coffee cup (Not much tea drinking here, it seems.) where cup sizes and designs are very important. Little mugs are not in vogue. The phrases on the mugs should be catchy or outrageous but not offensive. It is definitely not in style to praise your boss or your work. Being leisurely and environmentally concerned are considered very cool, here. The joke, here, is that the corporation is sending a liberal message as opposed to the politicians who are always espousing their conservative dogma. Is this a balancing act, or what? No, you play your part, and I will play mine; how is that for cooperation?

At this meeting, everyone is on a first-name basis and information is very important, so is your mug. The immigrant had information, but no mug. She was just another strange person on the block with little or no power. As the 'Mugless One' surveyed the group, the meeting commenced with everyone simultaneously taking a studied and practiced sip from their mugs.

The engineering manager started the meeting with good news by saying: "We are announcing the release of the Cytron.67 project. This is a successor to the QRS.57, 64-bit, lossless-compression module that had caused such a stir in the market place three years ago. This effort will avoid proliferation of the standard XX.57, which is built on the 8XY server's protocol to minimize techno-stress for our end users. We are all certain that this type of platform will enhance our plug-and-play capability and win us more market shares. Our marketing strategy this time is to decrease our timeline to market, thereby capturing the window at an earlier date…"

Someone in the audience asked, "What about the patent infringement problem with Question R Corp?"

All heads turned to the direction of the interloper. The crowd's breathing rhythm changed abruptly into one massive, combative, rainbow-colored, single-headed dragon, with numerous probing multi-colored eyes. There were a studied, more controlled, opening of the nostrils and a clenching of the jaws, as the miniature United Nations went to its primitive animalistic roots and decided to cross racial and ethnic lines and economically survive as one. Not a word was spoken, but the mood was, "Do not give us any bad news, now. We really mean it!"

The immigrant momentarily lost control and whispered her thoughts, saying, "Is this the real world?"

Her voice sounded like an explosion in the stillness of the room. The slow motion of all facet of life, coupled with the impregnated and contemplative stillness of the dimness of the room, changed into a giant sigh. The audience laughed and cheered the immigrant for being on their side. The suave techno-guru on the podium smiled and calmed the edgy crowd by giving them the word from one of his legal friends. Telling them, that the Question R Corp will work with us to avoid a patent battle, because Tom (one of the whereas-whereas boys), here, finally made them see the light—that they are infringing on *our* patent.

"What did you bring to their attention, Tom?" asked a well-attired jubilant-type with an affable, but commanding, voice from the edge of the podium. "This is one of the real power brokers," whispered a mentor to the wild-eyed, impressed immigrant. "He is our VP dealing with corporate strategy." A real VP, thought the immigrant who had heard of those types of power brokers before.

Tom continued, "...brought clause 15, subsection a, paragraph 2 of our contract which specifically spells out the terms and conditions under which the partnership should operate…in doing so, they had to abide by policies laid down in our last meeting…"

"Really?" smiled the aware immigrant. It seems that Mr. Tom, who is not her Uncle Tom by any stretch of the imagination, had come to a compromise in their last meeting to avoid a long and costly legal battle.

All facet of life seems to return to normalcy with this announcement. People were extolling the capabilities of their upper-level management to take them over the bumpiness of their latest corporate challenge. The immigrant looked around and was truly mystified. She had never before been in such a contemplative and competitive environment where people acted so civil but were definitely bent on war in all phases of the market place. Today, she learned the rule of this new dynamic melting pot of a culture: "I will compete with you to the death for what you have that I want. The smile on my face is not an indication of how I feel. It is my working uniform and nothing else!"

She muttered to herself, "These people are war-boats."

Mankin winked and smiled at the description. Where had he heard that saying before? Someplace, in the far recesses of his mind, that was a popular saying. He knew the origin of it was the description of ladies who were called *viragoes*. Not that they were actually viragoes, but they would rock the social order, and they were determined to get justice for themselves. After the meeting everyone seemed more animated and unwilling to lose the euphoric feeling. Her new friends came over, shouting that some of their friends **are** coming to visit her "cube." Now, the baffled immigrant wondered if she had one of these *cubes*. A period of silence ensued while she looked at her well intention, but quietly expectant, new friend whom asked if that was all right.

The new girl on the block had to come clean by saying, "What is *my cube*?"

"Your office! You frightened me in believing you wanted no visitors."

"Oh, yes, come visit my office. My "cube," too… Come on… you are welcome…"

They all gathered around hugging her, giving various information:

> "Aren't we a dynamic group?"
> "Let's go for a brewsky after this."
> "Remember, we wear our grubbys on Fridays."

Now, the New One is thinking: "cube," I now know, but what are **brewsky**, and **grubbys?** Very nice, well-mannered people, but with strange usage of the English words. Now, they are giving her advice when dealing with their production staff: "Be careful when you are dealing with the real people in the real world. Some can be very nasty, and they are important. Very important, too; they pay your salary." Real people are assemblers and other support personnel. *So, what am I?* she thought. The advice continued: "…so whenever dealing with them carefully plan, implement things, and watch them unfold…"

The Migrant One was startled to know she was not in the real world. She was just a visible technocrat, momentarily earning a good salary in a high-tech environment, where circumstances and alliances changed too rapidly to contemplate any form of job longevity in any one of these workplaces.

Mankin now wondered, "If this is not the real world, then where is the Real World? Where does reality live? **Let's take a real trip there...**

The scenery and landscape rolled by as the rickety bus negotiated dangerous hairpin curves on narrow, hilly, two-lane roads. The roaring of the engine, along with the timely blasts from the air horn, call one's attention to the difference in traveling in a Third World (or what is now called a developing) country, relative to the industrial ones. Looking at the expanse of cultivated lands with the carefree roaming of domestic animals shows the connection of people to the land. This is very unlike the disconnection of highly developed countries where people wearily live like monkeys on a tree. They are too wary to approach the ground (our homeland) for their essential sustenance of water and other minerals. These substances define us as humans—food, water, and the requirement to roam freely without obstruction. Instead, we live like shut-ins in high rises, slums, and other synthesized cyber-space apartments, with their controlled gadgetry to give the eternal false security from the prowlers (and the crawlers outside). Yeah, let us shut ourselves in. That is shut out the world—the environment—and seek solace in our loneliness. Let's take an escape from reality to the imaginary. Let's surround ourselves with technological gadgetry, because the enemy is at the door. But wait, on which side of the door is the enemy? And, which side is outside. After your brilliant dreams of yester-year turned into this present, boring nightmare, you watch the phone for hours each day hoping to hear the sounds of friends; especially those who call in the accent of your childhood. Sometimes, any accent will do, even the accents of the jaded voices of acquaintances of your adopted country. Beggars at times may not be "choosers." You are not too choosy anymore, "just call. Please!" As you stay behind the door of your house (not really a home), wondering which side of the door gives more fun and/or security, you play the scenes leading up to your present predicament—toys without joys! Is this what it is all about? All these years you planned for this crippling mortgage, the troubling body pain, the guilt-ridden dependency on legal drugs, and now this—disillusionment between your civilized walls. Where did you go wrong? Who is inside? At this stage have you (Who me? Yes, you!) ever thought of the fun you had before acquiring all these toys? Would you do it differently, with your prior lover(s), if you could bring them along with you, then? What do you think the result would have been, if you had stayed with them? Just think, it would be much happier for you now; but would you prefer to have given up your present toys for a chance at a different life with one of those whom you had rejected in your past love life? Have you seen any of these past admirers recently? If so, did you rejoice at your decision or were you saddened to see the toothless wonder from days gone by? No, one cannot go back home. There can be no going back home. March forward to a different reality in the similar place but at a different time. As the old-time bus conductor used to say, "Look so...forward!" And, the bus moves on; so does life.

Simnally looked through the daily newspaper with finality and uttered in a preaching tone, "The free market is a global strategy of the industrialized controller group to place the world under their domination without using military might, because that now would be too expensive."

"If the **USSR** had tried the free-market system, they would be better off now?" replied a smiling Kenworth.

"They are trying it now, and look what has happened to them!" smiled Simnally.

"They are going through growing pains."

"You mean, their death throes while the economists ring their death knells."

Kenworth replied, "If they had tried the free market long ago, they would be better off."

"They would be suffering for a longer time."

"What are you, Simnally, some throwback-type of communist?"

"Remember that Jesus the Christ was for the community. Right modern-day, Caiphas?"

"Come now, Simnally; don't try to tell me that Caiphas was a merchant!"

"Kenworth, you must understand what happened after the "removal of the free marketeers or racketeers" from the temple, that their protectors in the religious hierarchy orchestrated the removing of the Leader of the grass-roots movement. You know who the Leader is, don't you, my little 'free market racketeer'?"

"Simnally, it's like you are saying that the Divine One was crucified because he opposed the free-market strategy. What type of foolishness is this?"

"There is nothing as free market, Kenworth. Ask the millions of slaves from Africa or the present-day sweatshop workers. Talk with the people from countries that are burdened by the oppressive financial burdens of loans from the International Monetary Fund (IMF) and the World Bank. I know everything has its price, but some prices are just too high."

"Agreed, Simnally, but we as the controlled people need to manage our affairs better. We need to plan for the future generation's happiness. That means we have to open our own businesses to maximize profits for our growth."

"You want us to get into a more selfish attitude, or as the present day business gurus would say, 'do it with a win-win attitude'?"

"Simnally, on a serious note, there is no *them* and *us*. We are all one."

"Kenworth, you were never good at counting. Now, you have started to count the controller group as one with the oppressed group. The sad problem with you is that you really believe it. You failed to realize that information is the mainstay (the backbone) of power. It was always so, and it will remains so, especially if you failed to acknowledge that we, as a group, cannot make any decision for our own betterment until we get our people to understand that self-respect, knowledge, and economics are powerful tools of freedom. And, why are we always looking for a Messiah to give us something free or lead us out of what we conceived as our present-day Babylon. Perhaps we need to create our own Babylon! They killed all the Messiahs that come in peace, so perhaps we need another approach. A Deliverer who is willing to literally fight their type of fight…"

"Sounds like what the Jews were looking for during the pre-Christian days. You mean a Messiah to avenge them!"

"We need no paper-lion. We've had them before. Very ineffective for us…"

"So now, Simnally, you want to change history, and have your own "Babylon" as the Oppressors did? A pay-them-back for all those past tribulations…"

"So what is wrong with that notion, Mr. Apologists? Now, you think I am in a vengeance mode, but you did lament with me during the long oppression in South Africa. How come all of a sudden you forgot everything? A typical slave offspring…not much memory when dealing with the slave masters."

"Simnally, the Bible says…"

"Says what! Our people shall be slaves… 'or slaves obey your masters' …"

"Who is your master, Simnally?"

"The Creator…you think he sees the suffering…or he planned it all?"

"For us to suffer!" The younger man shook his head and exclaimed with a touch of anguish to his voice, "No, Simnally, you really can't believe that."

"Oh, master race apologists, do you now know the Master's plan for us, too?"

"Look at all the people around us; you cannot seriously believe we are placed here just to suffer…"

"I didn't say I believe we are here to suffer, and what is it with this number of people. Perhaps the number of people is the problem."

"The Bible says we should be fruitful and multiply, and that is the nature of things."

"If you want to be fruitful, go and plant food to minimize famine among our people. To multiply, use a pencil or a calculator; it is safer and sometimes more enjoyable in the long run. You read too much in other people's history in the biblical Old Testament. Next you are going to tell me that 'your' Creator tells you to plunder, rape, and enslaved other people when you envy their belongings."

"Follow your heart, Simnally... People will always have children..."

"Try telling me now that quantity has a quality all its own."

"Simnally, is this Mao's thoughts revisited here? Man, you are getting jaded."

"Kenworth, you don't believe in quality. You are too overwhelmed with quantity. Are you from South Africa? They won the battle, not by sheer numbers but with quality people who decided to win this one."

"No other country helped them, Simnally; be serious here."

"Yes, they did by voting against them in the Security Council, thereby uniting the population to fight as one. Anyway, they won the battle, but the war is yet to be won..."

"You still see more fighting there, Simnally? Ha. Ha. Ha...don't answer we all know what's going to happen after Mandela..."

"Ha. Ha. Ha...but must!"

"We all know procrastination is more like a preconditioning in a Third World country..."

"And, you are not talking about the social attitude this time, Simnally the Strokes!"

Mankin listened, but not with alarm, because he himself knew that the battle is not over. It is not easy to have the well-fed and satisfied predator bed down with the young aching prey. Such condition always ends in a chase, whenever the predator is hungry again. The prey cannot forget this episode. Perhaps the friends are correct about "procrastination" before explosion. Perhaps there is a tendency to forget inhumane treatment when one's belly is full. Is it especially so among the short-sighted, Oppressed group? They failed to learn from history or teach their history to their young.

By their failing to learn, the immigrants often abnegated their responsibilities to the commercial fable weavers on the television screen, by making excuses of working too many jobs, believing multiple jobs are an absolute necessity for happiness. Could it be they really think they are characters in the *Living Colors* sit-com? You may work all the multiple jobs you want, but the end result is how you planned your life. The quality of living is all that counts— the wellness of the spirit, if you will. Workaholic immigrants should remember the old island story of the cow and the horse. It seems that the cow takes it mellow by reminding herself that the "*Backra's* work is never done."

The horse on the other hand runs at a brisker pace saying, "It must done, it must done." Therefore, it spends an entire lifetime, tediously running, trying to complete an eternal task. Be industrious, but stop and smell the roses sometimes; don't be an ass.

One aware immigrant pointed this dollar-chasing attitude to her friend who was always leaving her child to do some "other job" to earn the extra few cents after taxes. The workaholic friend testily replied. "You wanted me to stay home and tell him about some silly Anancy stories…that spider is always robbing, or trying to deceive people…he is lazy and conniving, with no integrity. These are tales from Africa where women do all the work, while lazy men sit by and preen themselves. No wonder no development takes place there!" After this rebut she took her child to a cathedral where a sculpture depicted a suffering lion whose side was pierced by a lance. The wounded lion lay on his shield dying while he pleaded for the world to repent and sow the seed of respect and love. Now, we were all children before. (At least we hope so! Someone said there are exceptions to every rule. OK, let's exit, here.) Anyway, the child only sees this sculpture as a cartoon character to be loved and played with. Is this the message that was intended by the sculpture? Perhaps it is. Some artists are a bit far-out—weird, if you will! Not the cartoon part of course, but then again who can tell? The parent saw the sculpture in other ways. More with a religious fervor, possibly as Jesus the Christ in agony, pleading from the cross for humanity to repent and live in harmony. As the child continued playing with the sculpture, referring to it in endearment as the "Lion King," the quiet, embarrassed parent looked around, trying her best to remove the errant young one from using the sculpture to externalize a childish love to a favorite cartoon character. Mankin was amused when he remembered that people see art in different ways. He was also glad that this was not the era of the Catholic dominance, when the Inquisition killed at will; the poor little child could have been burnt at the stake as another heretic! We can imagine some *faithful* priests from the Dominican Order (or Franciscan friars) putting the poor child in an Iron Maiden and shouting, "Confess your sins that you are a spawn of Darkness!" Don't be a religion apologist, here, believing that would not happen, because the child could not have learned about the Lion King, then, because they had no TV. Remember that Iscariot was not watching TV's *Let's Make a Deal* when he betrayed the Anointed One!

A beautiful Mexican senorita silently came across and stood there in silence, looking at the struggling party trying to remove the unwilling child from the sculptured lion. She tacitly acknowledged their efforts, then dropped a bombshell by saying, "He is refusing to acknowledged the beast as a form of the male-Sky God. Don't rush it; give him some time. His emerging macho ways will finally bring him around!"

The surprise on everyone's face was tremendous. A vocal and dissatisfied Catholic customer in the store! Anyway, what is art except playthings to fantasize about? One person's art is another's plaything. Art is escapism. Perhaps the child wanted to "personalize the sculpture, that is to personalize art as a friend in need." This is a not too modern an approach, but he will eventually have to follow the rules by worshipping the "male Sky God," as most feminists are fond of saying when they lamented the rise of the patriarchy under the Catholic Dominion. The astonished onlookers **started laughing** as if surprised to hear her criticizing what is viewed as her heritage's religious icon. We know how people from a certain island admire the Mexicans. If you don't believe it; just try to remember the events with the Reggae Boyz Football team in a certain country. Gracious people remember, and they weep, too, for the Mexican team during the loss in the World Cup. Our CONCACAF group champions did put up a good fight. Thank you for the memories, Mexico.

While walking down the streets in Guadalajara with the brothers in Tlaquepaque [Te-la-ki-pa-ki], having a tequila for victory and friendship sake, Mankin **realized the Mexicans are** kind, spiritual, and gracious people with a strong sense of respect. Although reading the media in the US, one would not think so. This is a good place to live with beautiful and vivid artworks which tell stories. Good food abounds! The annoyed senorita really gave the laughing group an earful about the political turmoil and identity crisis she was facing. She had escaped to a place she called "the desert" to find some spiritual solace and personal growth among her friends. The disillusion of living in a country where the institutions are still in flux after all these centuries wore heavily on the beautiful and impetuous young leftist woman. She saw no end to the haphazard existence where her country is always considered a "second fiddle" on the international scene. Many times, she mentioned her "giant neighbor" to the north as the stifling giant who had played the role of the benevolent dictator so many times that she wondered if her nationality really counted. She lamented her role of a lonely female in a hyper-machismo, paternal society. She wondered about trade partnership in the NAFTA TRIAD as she called it. She explicitly avoided discussion on personal relationship with others, but her gripe about...

The condition to get things done without the stifling heavy-handed bureaucracy, with its redundancy procedure where everyone is afraid to make a decision unless their palms are "greased," selling out their identities to the highest bidder...

Mankin sees this as a universal lamentation of poorer countries. If only the poor lady knew that poorer countries all have this suffocating old ways of doing things. It is often said that in any country where government procedures are not effective in giving timely results, then corruptive ways to bypass them are always the method used to get the desired results. Perhaps the beautiful senorita should try getting a birth certificate on one of these Islands! Nothing is new here, senorita. People have to live somewhere, in some way, or die trying for a better life. Now, we certainly know why migration is desirable for some people. But is it better? To have choices is to grow. Migration is a growing choice.

Mankin tried to compare the immigrant's lifestyle in Canada and the USA with those of Europe. In trying to be objective, he missed so many points that he decided to listen to them talking about their old country of origin. In most cases the conclusions were that they missed their old countries and even more so as the years go by. Their new realization is that every lifestyle has its value, and no one place can give total happiness... So just enjoy the journey through life. This seems to be the worthwhile message to learn.

He noticed some glaring inconsistencies with immigrants' solidarity within the urban areas of large Canadian cites like Toronto in comparison to US cities. The US ethnic groups have a much stronger bond of togetherness forged in centuries of hardship of fighting a common enemy with high visibility. This solidarity is especially entrenched among the older and wiser groups who will always acknowledge each other on the streets with various kinds of greetings. Their Canadian counterparts are still practicing "tribalism," a type of *divisive Tutsi-Hutu* mentality with their petty sense of colonial aloofness, which stems from insecurity and vestiges of parochial attitudes from their old countries. They still have not comprehended the idea that they are a "small fish in a big pond." They just stare at each other balefully as if to say, "get out of my way, or I will run you over." Perhaps many of them should recognize that they are just standing still; being very stagnant, therefore they are incapable of running over anyone; they are more prone to trip themselves.

The migrant people from the Caribbean have practiced this type of social exclusion so effectively that they hardly ever speak to each other on the streets. Then again there are people from individual islands who hated other groups with a vengeance. Mistrust, here, is fierce! Mankin watched as the migrant ethnic groups from Africa and Asia met the Western immigrant groups, especially those from the Caribbean islands. He marveled at the undercurrent of mistrust among all groups, both new and old arrivals, as they competed for their share of the small "doled piece of pie that dropped from the subsidy table." Here racism and ethnocentrism bred serious mistrust and hatred. It pitted powerless groups against each other in their struggle for survival in a strange land where political rhetoric is smooth and where big businesses and special-interest groups lobbied for dominance at the immigrants' expense.

All migrant groups tend to classify rather than include, developing some powerless hierarchical and exclusionary social structure, which excludes other island groups. Listen to some of their silly little reasons— "They eat chicken feet in cooked cornmeal." "Chicken is nasty." "They scratched in the mess." "Them even stabbed crab, and then cook it; a group of mad, crab-stabbing murderers. Nobody should go to their homes." "Man you eat crab! That's wild Anancy.

Boy, people can't eat that!" "Woman you eat snake! Rass, gal, no wonder you can't get any man; you cold blooded. Give me a wide circle, Ms. Ananconda, ...just watch out for the mongoose." "You eat susumber plant! Help me...you will put bad spell on mi ass, boy!" "You eat 'mountain chicken'? You will call bad blessings, and possibly volcanoes, down on mi head...croak off sister!" "You eat monkey? You practicing genocide...monkeys' facial expressions resemble people...you are evil." Mankin speculated whether anyone noticed that they all ate something that had been alive, and they, themselves, were alive and possibly seeking the same thing—food. Although many of their foods would not be included in Mankin's orthodox eating habits, he still would not have excluded anyone on a purely dietary choice...unless of course human bodies started coming up missing. Oops! Bear in mind this is no historical Carib joke. Mankin admired the Caribs, although the European historians claimed they were cannibals. Who generally wrote history, anyway—the winners of the conflict? Apparently, every group which shows defiance to slavery is always depicted as either uncivilized or as cannibals. Bear in mind the docility of the well praised and highly sympathized Arawak Indians never helped their plight either. Even more of them were killed. Is there a lesson here?

While Mankin smiled at the migrants' biases, he saw a youth walking in his urban "get up," which includes a big, oversized pair of black pants, hanging way down on his hips, with a comparable oversized dark coat, emblazoned with some positive environmental message about saving the planet. Under his coat, he wore a blue-checkered shirt, hanging outside his pants. He bounced along in his studied, cool, urban-choreographed-type of walk, with his arms hanging loose and rotating frontward with each low shoulder movement. Mankin smiled and wondered, "what being is coming his way." As the youth approached, Mankin observed that the young one wore the usual high-profile brand of sneakers, but he defied the traditional convention of urban image by wearing his cap with the peak pointing forward instead of backward.

He started talking to another dissimilar dressed youth with a cricket bat.

"You played cricket, 'High Up'?"
"No, we do not play cricket in Somalia."

"So what you doing with a cricket bat, African bro?"
"It's my Zimbabwean friend's bat. Can you play?"

"Yes. Perhaps I could even make the West Indies team if I tried hard," laughed the forward peaked youth.

"The former world champion?" asked the Somali youth with renewed interest.
"Anyway, that was then; this is the land of basketball, football, make that soccer, and tennis—with baseball the major sport at this time. So, man from Somalia, what is your sport?"

"Distance running is my thing, Western man"

Mankin watched with keen interest as two more youths, a Zimbabwean and a Trinidadian, joined the couple. The information was well laid back as the youths of the Western hemisphere, who obviously had been in Canada longer than their African counterparts, tried to "out cool" the latter.

"So you play cricket, and believed you could make the West Indies (W.I.)?" laughed the cool Trinidadian, looking over his small dark glasses, which hanged lowly on his nose.

At this time the Zimbabwean was standing erect and smiling, as if to say, "Are you joking? This caliber of cricketers is not in this area. You just don't meet them on the street." On the other hand the Somali was quite serious about the other two questioning his newfound friend's ability—a kind of, "how dare you questioned my friend's athletic prowess?"

"True, true."

"Are you a bowler or a bats?" inquired the Trinidadian still smiling.

"Max pace, at hyper speed, with optimum accuracy!" said the forward peak one.

"Possibly *fast* and *foolish,* too," suggested the cool, wiry Trinidadian, with a slight grin.

"Look, Lawd, you have a bat, and you can find out which of the f's am good at."

The Trinidadian quickly replied: "I am a spinner, boy; I ain't gonna let you beam me with a fast Yorker or bounce one to my head. Ah! Ah! We bowlers must stick together. Talk to the Zimbabwean; he owns the bat."

"What we have here is hemispherical politics, where you guys are ganging up on a brother from the East," shouted the laughing Zimbabwean.

The youths instantly changed their focus to a girl, dressed in tight black shorts, strolling across the grass. They all laughed together; and the Forward-peaked One philosophized, "If you keep on feeling in the 'slips,' then you may eventually get caught in the 'leg trap.' Remember this ain't cricket, now, man."

They all laughed together giving one another high fives as they walked away in one of those youthful discussions where everyone has nothing to say but everything to say simultaneously.

Mankin thought how easy it is to get along in a cross-cultural society, if we just try talking to each other. We should just try to understand that our relationship is much more than the face, the color, and the different states, and trends. It is impressive that the Caribbean groups can combine to play international cricket, and be World champions for about fifteen years, but cannot agree to respect each other in a new, and sometimes hostile, environment that sees all the groups as one type of people—a common interloper. Cricket showed the way to solidarity, long before CARICOM. Ever heard of the dangerous, and mesmerizing, Ram/Val combination? "Cricket lovely, cricket at…" possibly never heard of Lord Kitchener either. No, not the one with the imperial Boer War attachment! Well, what can one expect from a *non-roots,* latter-day foreign-born youngster, anyway? Well, why should we not expect the best from you? You have more information than we did. But, then do you use this information effectively? Anyway, North American athletes are quite different in their approach from Caribbean-based athletes.

Here we now have athletes from the same island foolishly cursing each other just to win media popularity. The frightful thing is they are already popular, but they choose to demonize others who have shown them the way to glory. We must try to understand each other's weaknesses. A kind word does not necessarily mean weakness. The immigrant, as a group, badly needs to learn and practice respect for each other. A kind word for a fallen hero does not mean you condone his action; nor, does it demean you if you agree with him. We all know how image conscious today's great athletes are. They have to be able to make a decent living, which they really deserve. Anyway, a kind word means you can understand mistakes. Remember the same System which praises you today will likely abandon you tomorrow by quickly disassociating itself from you and referring to you as the native of your birthplace. Even then your own native land, with your interest at heart, may unwillingly choose to be mute. This is to steer the correct political path to maintain close ties with a powerful and benevolent friend. This part of the *incident* may not be well known but that is the way it is (*interpreted?*). It has happened before. Remember! History? Sometimes one has to strictly adhere to the group mentality to keep "anti-social wolves" from his doors. Mankin is not recommending having a "hive mentality" but just to recognize the virtue of group dynamics to shelter us from the ever-popular, and well-connected, fringe groups. Sports is a great medium for national or racial cohesion. Yes, how about dem Reggae Football Men! Here all groups share an uncommon solidarity for the Reggae Team... Thanks, especially, to the wonderful friends (the radical group of **'baajans'**) from Trinidad. We knew you deserved to make it years ago but for a certain unworthy referee who connived and openly stole your glory. Your turn next island 'Soca Warrior' brothers from the Twin Islands.

The lasting virtue of the Reggae Boyz is the unsurpassed legacy of social cohesion. This is a time when even the criminals and police have a beer. In a certain incident, a group of opposing "gun persons" (there were women there with guns in their handbags, too. This mistaken idea about gunmen and not gun-women is a farce.

The women never generally get caught, because they know when to fade out.) While one group of gunmen shouted, "shoot man!" —meaning score a goal for our country—the other group immediately rushed for their weapons, believing it was **a** call to action. Some police quickly separated them, shouting, "Perhaps tomorrow!" Each group quickly returned to watching the game with their usual "coaching" tactics on how the players should react. Mankin breathed slowly, thinking how this interaction could be like one of those old-time showdowns between "the toughest" and "the roughest" in the west end of a certain Caribbean city. At least this time there is calmness. No one is jumping over fences with Molotov cocktails in each hand, and a dangling unlit, illegal, 'smokes' in their mouths, shouting, "Give the man a light, nuh!" Imagine having a flaming bottle-bomb in each hand and then having the nerve to scare non-smokers by asking for a light! Anyway, certain obvious things cannot be pointed out under certain conditions…this was one time. It is not considered wise, then, to tell the hostile bomber to use his own flame. He may misinterpret your good intentions and brand you as an enemy…understood?

As the beer flows and the spirit mellows, there appears a certain comradeship among everyone. The main surprise is that many of these people know each other. They all went to the same school with the police. Mankin wondered why these intercine wars among brothers were necessary. To hear them blaming the politicians and other people called **"dons"** was too ridiculous to mention. Everyone claiming the System contrived to take advantage of their economic scarcity. One quiet scholarly looking "outlaw" calmly espoused, "Man we have to take some responsibilities for our actions, or we will all die like dogs! It is a known thing that the politicians give our names to the police after the election when they cannot deliver on their promises to us.

Nothing new!" The quiet, Scholarly One then slowly took off his cap and unblinkingly looked the nearest policewoman straight in the eyes. The cop hurriedly reached for her beer without a reply. There was a deadly silence, except for the TV announcer… "He took a hard shot from just outside the penalty…" Mankin's spirit shuddered thinking, "So that is how it's done. The final closure!" While the island team of superb "warriors" struggled on the field, a slightly inebriated American intellectual asked, "Your country had been ruled by the British for over 300 years before your Independence, so why are you now working for the Spanish nobility to take over?" Silence. Apparently the term "don" means different things, to different people, at different times. The original Spanish don may have used Runaway Bay for their getaway, but today's "don" keeps the others in another "garrison" at bay with the help of those who presently want to confess to past cruelties, including murders. These high profile "Fathers-wish-to-be Confessors" caused all this tribalism. They chased people Overseas and polarized the country into little garrisons as they vied for their little slices of power. Someone possibly told them that "power came out of the nozzle of a gun."

They practiced that, and now, they believe the Reaper is shadowing them, so they all want to confess. What a farce! What will be their punishment? No one wants to address that. They still have a law against murder there; don't they? They want to get away with it like the Apartheid murderers in South Africa. What is going on, here, with this "talking the truth" business? Who is it helping except the *Fathers-wish-to-be-Confessors*…who get their feelings soothed before their last hurrah? These guys are disrupters of the human spirit; they murder people, too, so what is their punishment? Is it truth but no consequence, as usual, for government policy makers? Could it be their wishes to come out in the open and legally write books about their crimes? Perhaps we should enact a Nuremberg-type trial, but then the wanna-be Confessors, with their political allies, would have to give their approval. Imagine murderers deciding if the population can try them for murder. The poor guys in prison on death row have no such choice. A specific reason why capital punishment is questionable—it kills only the powerless within the population!

The greatest disservice of all is done when many islands combine and tell their compatriots that whenever they commit crimes to tell the authorities that they are from a specific island. In doing so, they undeservingly brand a whole generation of people as criminals, thereby giving an inclusiveness of criminality to one island. This type of shameful behavior caused the ultra right wing conservative hate-mongering media-types to heighten their attacks on a special island group as if saying they are all from the same *yard*; so, *"Yardies"* they all are! Then these other silly little idiots laughed believing they have accomplished a national feat in protecting their own little island country. Mankin pondered, "When will these migrants (no, we) all realize that they are one people linked in a social collective, struggling to be happy?" The System makes no difference about the little nation you came from. It sees only a special *characteristic*—a very definitive one too...the System is not island conscious; it is more hue conscious.

As Mankin pondered these social dilemmas, time and travelers quietly passed. Mankin glanced at the portrait of a Priestess on the magazine cover nearest to him. The picture depicted the goddess worshipped in an earlier period in Earth's history. Immediately, there was a commotion as a short sturdy woman with numerous bags and packages brusquely pushed her way through the quiet crowd. Her entourage was just as noisy and belligerent. Mankin gathered they were coming from some meeting or convention. They were feeling empowerment vibration to the hilt. The woman daringly glanced around at the males saying: "You know everything man designed he gave the male the best. The female washrooms are generally full, and the male sparsely populated."

Mankin calmly listened while thinking about the number of users per stalls and time duration per usage, but there is too much anger here to simplify this design problem.

"The phallus-type is a threat to everything that is human," replied a slender, blue-eyed beauty.

"We are the goddesses of this planet, and we can't even enjoy it. Just wait until we find a way to have only females. Males are so maladjusted," blurted a short haired feminist.

"Ladies you don't have to be so upset. You all live in a democratic society and have a vote. Just vote the men out of power, and have all the washrooms and all the 'no-men', or 'women' you need. Just leave me with some *good* men," shouted a smiling, dark-skinned woman.

All eyes from the feminist group were focused on the speaker. The rustling of hands on numerous bags, packages, and what-have-you fell silent. Other people stared at the boisterous group, and also, at the challenger from a different racial group, and possibly also, from a different social class.

Mankin immediately recognized the problem as a political one, because the feminist movement is trying to attract more of the less-privileged women of other racial groups to their cause as numbers signify more power for the leaders.

"What happened, sistah? You are afraid of the darker-skinned females?"

"No!" chorused the feminists in unison. "We are just surprised that you have broken the sisterhood circle by opposing us before all these men," explained the blue-eyed lady.

"Yes, I know that men in groups are dangerous, but we, the darker-skinned women, started to view the feminist movement as a type of inclusive female club for people of a special shade. People like me are the exclusive group, because I do not have your privileges."

"You seem to believe that we are anti-male, and would rather skew the creative juices to reflect a dominant majority of female births, but that is not the whole story," said the short feminist.

"So what's wrong with that?" murmured short hair.

"Everything. Fewer males would make them even more powerful—like gold or precious stones," explained the short feminist.

"Very good reasoning," Mankin chuckled, thinking if economic scarcity drives up the value of commodities, so it would be with a scarcity of the male commodity.

"I like the movement, but it became a centrist movement headed by privileged, intellectual, Caucasian-types who lost touch with many women of different shades with comparable ability. Are the groups now run by men?"

"What!" A group effort.

"We are not simpletons. We know that men in groups are dangerous. Take for instance; the Inquisition, the College of Cardinals, the Joint Chiefs of Staff, the Supreme Soviets, the…"

"How about the Ku Klux Klan?" mentioned dark-skin.

"How about the Twelve Apostles?" chided a male voice.

"What was the Apostles' uniform, Mr. Testosterone? All of those mal-adjusters have uniforms. Then, of course, there was Paul of Tarsus. Your Saint Paul," shouted blue-eyes as she glared in the general direction of the male voice.

"All of these uniformed male organizations practiced male dominance, and female exclusion, and have their religious dogma to back it up. Even if you are legally elected to these organizations, you may be denied a chair to sit with them. Even if you are their elected boss!" replied the short feminist.

"Sexism, as slavery, is a tool of institutional oppressions sanctified by the church, and other religious bodies," said dark-skin.

"And, men started all those," echoed short-hair.

"And, women keep using them to their benefit, especially sexism," said a male voice.

"You are proud of every injustice done to the environment, to the human spirit…the burning of your mothers as witches after they painfully gave you birth!" shouted an irate short-hair.

"No, but I like being a man, and I like my woman being a woman, too, and not being something else."

"Brother Dan, please don't get into it, please," pleaded a middle-aged man.

"What is this 'something else' you mentioned, sir? Your companion is a preacher?" inquired blue-eyes.

"Yes. He is a fine preacher, too."

"One of those who sees the female womb as subservient to the male phallus. You guys don't believe in equality in any form, hence the 'missionary-way,'" explained blue-eyes.

"He is your preacher? Well, well, a new twist to an old power game," laughed dark-skin.

"You don't believe in my ability to lead flocks of other racial groups?" shouted the angry preacher.

"Your ability is not under scrutiny, here, it is your straight-laced attitude, which sees women as low-class people, that offends me. How come there are none of the big churches that are willing to employ women preachers in any of those communities that you came from, although women make up a greater portion of your congregation?" dark-skin shouted, with a special, fierce body language.

"Why are you doing this?" replied the Reverent one.

"Reverend, don't talk to her," replied the brother of the flock.

"Your type is worst than the power brokers. You are very dangerous to women. He is better than you because we know where we stand with him," said dark-skin pointing to the church brother.

"What do you women want?" queried a voice from the crowd.

"How about happiness? Yes, happiness!"

"Then come to the Lord!" said the preacher with open arms.

"Who is going to lead us there? A man leading females to a male Sky-god," scornfully laughed blue-eyes.

"Men wrecked the world over these centuries. Do you really believe spiritual people trust anyone of you?" muttered the short feminist, as she looked at the preacher and the brother with an air of finality.

"You had the world first and look what happened...killing off young men in your yearly ritualistic marriages to your Earth Queen of Heaven-types. Not even knowing which male fathered your children," scornfully added an older intellectual-looking man.

"Whose body is it?" This was a well-organized committee response. It was plain they were organized to answer like this. A total silence grasped the whole area. The well-dressed, conservative gentleman was quite surprised. The airport security personnel came around to check out the disturbance. Dark-skin laughed, breaking the silence: "They sent some of their own kind, with a token one of us, to suppress freedom as usual." The lone Caucasian female in the security detachment stared at her companions, asking,

"What she means?" Her male companions tactfully looked away, quietly shrugged their shoulders, and walked away. The combatants stared at the departing security personnel...and continued.

"Yes, whose body is it, Mr. Professor?" asked short-hair, with studied calmness.

"It is your body, but we have an interest in it, too. Men and women complement each other. We are connected," calmly answered the intellectual looking man.

"Do you think I have an interest in your body? And, do you think I am connected to you, your ribs, or whatever?"

"The ribs part we can leave out."

"No, we will not leave that out!" shouted the Preacher.

Mr. Professor, shrugged his shoulders nonchalantly, as if telling him he may do as he pleased. The discussion from the feminists took on a more intellectual slant than before.

Men do not give birth...so why don't you go away after the sex act...you generally do anyway...so why do you want to have control over the female body when you have your own body...you are looking for personal possessions, not love or companionship...inventing a male deity to excuse your action...posing as protectors while slavery is your design...

"Men are natural protectors of women," echoed the church brother.

"Who told you that? The Indo-European doctrinaires when they destroy the Goddess worships or the Yahweh Boys with their Old Testament Levite priests when they overran Canaan and murdered all those people in the name of their Sky-god—even brutally stoning their own people for exhibiting a freedom of choice with their own bodies.

Or, is it the Catholic Christian Church leaders with their political slants to enslave humanity, especially women? You just want a vehicle to breed young males to be sent to war, thereby solidifying your position of power, and also, to have more women as possessions to play your sex games," intoned the smiling, slender, blue-eyed beauty.

"Think we are both reaping our different rewards for treatments meted out to each other in our past Millennium?" queried a very unruffled Mr. Professor.

The unbelievable happened; short-hair smiled, glanced at Mr. Professor, and turned away to stack her luggage. Did they know each other?

Mankin remembered someone defining gender war as some extreme intellectual flirtation that is generally settled physically on the median plane.

S. Egroeg Reklaw

REALITY CHECK

Mankin stood there looking at yesterday's living area, now covered with tall trees and dense vegetation, leaving no visible trace of its former inhabitants. He finds it hard to believe that his old world could have vanished without leaving any physical trace to attest to his former connection with this place. He ponders, "How thoughtless can one be in thinking that nature will justify one's existence by leaving intact untended structures?" As Mankin gazed at the tall, sturdy trees emerging over the tangled vegetation, he started to compare the steep hill with the gradient of yesteryear. He wondered if the steepness of the hill grew with the surrounding vegetation. He could believe in the natural principle that the quantity of tombs in the grove increased with the number of years. There were tombs and a very special one with its rough inscription, giving only the year of death and a simple remembrance message. No name was inscribed; it was unbelievable to conceive that the writer could remember the date but not the name. Could it be that the *inscriber* was good at writing numbers but not alphabetical characters? This is not a joke, because in the hazy recesses of his mind, Mankin recollects the local village lawyer, Mr. Natty, who was somewhat of a social gadfly. He was present at all functions, funeral and Nine Nights included. This is the same Mr. Natty who signed his name on a document before the local police sergeant. When he was asked what type of signature was that, he boldly answered that he told the policeman before he signed that he cannot read, but he can write. So, how can he now expect him to read what is on the paper? Those were simple and enjoyable days...perhaps Mr. Natty's legacy is still around here? Mankin paused to remember voices, faces, mannerisms, and acts of love from an adult who once walked among us. And, there was this very special area where another love one rests. He heard voices of loved ones paying their last respect in one of those sad funeral songs, saying farewell for all eternity. This time there were no singing voices. The present voices were those of the present migrant generation, questioning, with deference, what it was like back then! It was good to know that the new generation cares and chooses to be connected to the generation long passed. The singing voices were finally still, the circle had been made, and a new generation began. Mankin knew, then, that this was no longer his physical world to replay his mind's video in the tangled grove. His friends had long ago moved on to another unseen reality, beyond a veil he presently cannot pierce.

There is, now, no well-trodden path to climb the hilltop as it was then—an indication that a generation had passed although memory remains fresh. It is nature's way of telling man that he should know his limitations, because nature will not modify its course for an individual (or, will it?) The terrain looked similar, but the faces and voices changed. Names stand still, but time is continuous. Mankin looked at the new generation, mentally blessed him for his observation, respect, and understanding of Mankin's past life, then physically turned and walked away, while still listening to the voices of a more carefree day calling him to come back and play again. As he moved away along the narrow country tract, a flood of memories rushed toward the surface when he passed the place where he last saw the face of his loved one before she left him for all eternity. As he re-played the events of those simpler times, the sadness dissipated into a feeling of childish ecstasy. Just remembering friends who wanted to experience the level of ecstasy which comes with adolescent desires, when parents are too busy, concerned with more trying circumstances during the Set-up or the 9TH Night! Yes, he now plainly remembers this was a time when young ones seek forbidden companionship, during the darkness, when social rules were relaxed through grief. Mankin can still hear the cultural dirge from the thatched booth; "…from mi come ya mi no drink no white rum. Mi ah go tear down the booth and go 'way…' Ritualistically threatening to tear down the booth and leave if the singers were not given another round of food and strong drinks. Yes, it was sad, then, but now, the Seasons have moved on, and Mankin knows there is a time when

"We shall meet, by and by!"

He mentally waved good-bye to a place he once enjoyed, as the setting sun signaled its good-bye by slowly sliding behind darkened dragon-shaped clouds as it retired the cooling landscape to darkness; leaving a scattered reddish palette of light rays among the various cloud patterns. In the not so far distance, Mankin saw the ominous, blackened shape of a low-flying aircraft, silhouetted against the dimly lit skyline. It came into view, traveling silently on a parallel course to the earth, as if on a strafing run to immobilize an enemy's city, just before the roar of its engine pierced the twilight stillness. It is evening, and it is time to catch a local bus to another destination. As Mankin watched the densely packed buses pass, he marveled at the level of expertise of the passengers as they swing to-and-fro to steady themselves while holding onto the handrails. The ride is a "get-personally-acquainted-with-each-other-while-being-fully-attired" one. Other things are also exchanged—perfumes and attitudes. The conductor has a language all his own, and this is changeable with his mood. One constant is the driver's ability to understand the conductor's every language change.

"Look so!"

The bus moved as the conductor shouted his order. He then encouraged the passengers to "move down" in the aisle. Mankin diligently looked for the imaginary space but could find none. However, he observed the action of a young lady, dressed in yellow, having a slender man in an unwilling, traveling embrace from the rear. The poor modest-looking fellow was trying his best to defend himself by squeezing his thin frame between a seat and a column. The lady had him firmly pinned among the passengers with the help of the moving vehicle. He was trapped in a corner, and the undulating ride became a "marriage" as her bouncy mammary glands played ping-pong with the smaller man's face. Apparently, she was aware of his difficulties, because she defiantly glared (**"wrenched!"**) at him for a short while, as he squirmed in his little mobile trap, while trying to put a decent, or civilized, distance between them. After many "slaps" to the face and "bounces" to the body, he finally gave up on his futile flirt with civility; settling into a more comfortable ride. Even then, he was not doing too well, because his face mirrored his nervousness with perspiration cascading down. He made the mistake of trying to remove his little handkerchief from his pocket and stepped into the greatest embarrassment of the whole ride, perhaps of his entire life! He tried squeezing his hand in his pocket only to find that his' captor's ample thighs surrounded his pockets. **He nervously had his hand between her thighs!** She nonchalantly raised her eyes to the heavens as if questioning his ability to do things well, calmly turned him around as if she was about to administer a spanking, then helped him to put his hand in his own pocket. He fumbled, then finally succeeded in removing a white handkerchief from his right side pocket and nervously wiped his perspiring brow. The lady calmly watched, sighed, then quietly shook her head and smiled at his efforts to be comfortable as the bouncy ride continued. He tried to be bold, by looking into her eyes before replacing his saturated, little, moist rag in his pocket.

Mankin theorized the Nervous One needed a large towel, not a small fancy looking perfumed rag. After wiping his face, he steadfastly looked into her eyes, as if contemplating the provocative attitude of this daring woman. She continued staring at him, as if daring him to openly speculate about his new traveling arrangement. His pupils dilated (not constricted as if he was in agony) as if he were having an ecstatic experience. As the simmering fluid continued pouring from his body, he quietly, and almost obediently, removed his little hanky, and again, wiped his face under the calm and calculating scrutiny of his tormentor, whom must now appear to him as the brazen, but contented, Amazon. It was obvious that his body was damped but certainly not his spirit. He was fighting back the only way he knew how, giving her a penetrating stare, as if saying, "Woman I know your game!" Mankin knew the lady understood the communication. The Nervous One was telling her he was now under stress, trying to be decent, but he was not the "Heavenly Donkey"-type of a husband who has to cringe and obey a woman's every command. He was not the "yes-dear-I-agree-with-whatever-you-say" type. The lady smiled brightly, as if in agreement, while she stepped closer to him and resumed their previous "connections." Well, some people have to take their pleasures wherever they can. "Ride on!"

The "ride" continued until they reached the place called Town. A place where it is said that many returning "wrongdoers" reside. The "wrongdoers" were returning after decades of pillages and murders in North America and Europe. These crimes were often committed under the scheme of justice, or pure criminality, and also by "political enforcers" who were spirited away from the island by their political organizations. Now, there are other foreign wrongdoers called "Deportees," young ones, too, with nowhere to go. They had no root structure, no ideas, and no spiritual connection to a place they left during infancy—a place that their parents once called home. In their spiritual and social disconnection, they wondered around like zombies among a strange, indifferent, and derisive populace. At the tourist areas and large towns, they gathered, watching the international transportation depart (without them, of course) to lands they remembered so well. Lands of glittering fashions, rapid and efficient transportation systems, an abundance of good food, the latest in high-tech industries, the best in medical technology, and many good schools (which most of them foolishly avoided.) A place where ironclad institutional controls and orders are enforced by uniformed enforcers with the newest technological devices that put the population under a tight control with the dreadful, but effective, **numbering system**. Now, most of the younger ones walked about as if in a daze, listening to the jeering voices of passersby, as if wondering how fate has dealt them such a hard blow. The older ones, who left during adolescence or adulthood, have a slight advantage, but a cautious and long-suffering population still does not accept them. Some of the latter have seen changes that put their lives in danger for a change…their former political bosses lost power over the decades. (Many of these politicians are now playing the trendy new wanna-be Father Confessors' role.) Or, the Deportees have become an embarrassment, and quite likely, were wanted by the authorities, too! These "operators" were in peril from their former bosses, the new power guys on the block, the more aggressive justice system, their victim's families, and even associates who can be cheaply bought to settle old scores. Now, trapped in a past criminal life and surrounded by water, there is presently no escape…except…what?

Now, the computer-age, with its binary "zeros and ones" —or is it logic— "high or low" has finally caught up with them and matched them a low blow…now there is nowhere to hide from the high resolution, high speed, "wideband scanner." Some are even seeking mercy and a chance to return Overseas by giving away friends' and relatives' criminal secrets to their former homelands. "Ways of the destructors!" uttered an old street vendor, as he watched a group of young, gold-toothed 'Returnees' scrounging a living on the dusty streets. As Mankin look at the changing infrastructure of the once vibrant **old Parade Square** of the place **called Town,** he noticed people huddling closely under a big tree, under pizzas, or other makeshift shelters. They were sheltering from a tropical rain while awaiting transportation from the big city to their homes. Instantly, a man, a silent marauder, passed by. His very presence gave the knowledgeable city-dwellers a warning of impending danger, like the action of hens during the presence of a marauding mongoose. In this case, reactions were silent but just as intense…an inner scream!

His probing, green eyes were like piercing laser lights, coming from the head of a venomous viper in one of those scary science fiction movies. His elongated head was on firmly built square shoulders, and he had a slender, brown frame of about five-feet-ten and about 180 pounds. He scanned his preys across the Square with the clinical precision as robots checking a material for defects or weak spots. His blue denim pants and soft, multi-colored shirt was like a camouflage to help a predator to easily blend with his populous surroundings. Apart from his eyes, the other outstanding physical attributes were his long, strong, slender fingers. They were well prepared; they were special tools of his trade. The super-pickpocket was on the prowl, similar to a lonely panther in the early hours before sundown after a heavy downpour of rain. He was like any hungry predator on the Serengeti Plain during the dusk hours—a last chance for the day.

"Lickah!" shouted an anonymous voice from the crowd.

The hunter stealthily moved away without even looking to see who raised the alarm. He knew the game was up, and there would be other times, other preys. Mankin watched the pickpocket with the mesmerizing stare move away. He pondered how many honest souls had this predator robbed. He heard voices of women crying with despair in small distant villages when they discovered their valuables had been lost after they had spent months of toil to sell their crops in the town. He even saw the eyes of small children, peering in the darkness at their parents, with bewilderment as they tried their best to understand what had happened to the candies and other simple goodies that they usually received from their mother. Mankin thinks about man's inhumanity to each other as he traveled away to a rural locale where time seemed to stand still. In this rural village named British, the place is as remote as the ruling imperialistic Britons are removed from their poor colonial subjects—a brutish descent down a rough meandering road to an under shrubs of sparse vegetation to the area of a vanishing lifestyle—a marginal, and nightmarish, agricultural existence of yesteryear—a place where time takes a break to survey past travails. Here lives only those whose energy are in transitory stages—the very young who cannot leave or the old and tired whose desire is just to rest and watch time stand still. Nothing seems to break the dreary monotony except the ever-changing light and shadows of night and day. More like a deathwatch! Here resides some of the "**home guards,**" those that had never ventured across the seas to seek a different living in a foreign land. Mankin watched a typical "home guard," appearing, now, more like a hermit since his family had left him years ago...or is it vice-versa? Mankin believes living here is not just a physical endurance routine; it has to be a mindset, which plays havoc with the resonance of the infinite light within us, the very soul itself.

The wiry gray haired hermit was a jovial and shirtless wonder who had dropped out of society for decades. Now, from under a cool shade tree, he watched the approaching party and smiled a greeting **of** recognition at his daughters. He was even more dumbfounded to realize that a brother and a nephew were among his visitors; also a social rebel (whose family spanned almost a century of friendship). The contented hermit smiled, remarking that in antiquity he remembered a brother by that name. The visitor looked around too and viewed over a 40-year time lapse in architecture, where tombs dotted small plots as testimonies to their past inhabitants—the happy homemakers of years gone by. This habitat of the removed ones were not dilapidated but exuded a sense of tiredness; all the vibrant energy had been steadily drained away over years of marginal existence. The once beautiful gardens were in ruins, as weeds and other weathering agents reclaimed once luxuriant plots. The unpainted windows with their soiled and parted, tattered curtains begged for speculation of their last active inhabitants. Mankin looked at the windows wondering who parted these curtains and why? It was as if their past old and tired inhabitants had made a valiant effort to glance at the sunlight for one last time before lying back and expiring into oblivion; a last **farewell to this mortal existence.** The contemplating hermit became animated and slipped into a talkative mode. He put on his small orange-colored, tailored shirt, which had been draped around his neck. He then stood erect and offered his warm hospitality of good fruits, water coconuts, and "smokes" for his friend, the social radical, but he was very specific about no "smokes" for his family, especially his younger generation. His emphasis on this point makes it sounded like a hermit's decree. Mankin realized the **"Hermit One"** was protective of the younger generation. He was maintaining a respect level that had left the immigrant groups when they migrated Overseas to seek their wealth. All throughout their conversation, Mankin marveled at the good body structure, the clear brown eyes, and the easy bouncing strides of the well-conditioned older man. There definitely is something good everywhere; a person just has to find it, the key to happiness. The thing about that is how do you know it when you find it? Is the search still on for you? Mankin posed the question, "Are there many immigrants who are now ready to come back to this condition?" He was aware that n**ew** technology and globalization had marginalized many of the older, unskilled immigrants. **Do they that** badly want to leave the great misery of the exclusionary environment and the mean streets, now that they are all older and have medical problems, possibly arising from their long and stressful **industrial heritage? What a choice!**

While the little group said their many farewells, Mankin wondered if they would ever again meet the lonely hermit in such a cordial manner. There were a few promises—wishes—about the future. There were also nostalgic exchanges of earlier times when parents were young and the children were vibrant with little of life's cares. The question arises, "Shall we see each other again in this world?" No one wanted to answer, as they looked at old familiar surroundings of little house surrounded by graves and covered with partially withering flowers—all in remembrance of their long-departed loved ones. Their eyes misted over while the visiting group drove away, away from this happy place of yesterday; trying their best to retain the kinder images of a past, a happier time without actually glancing back at the present, depressing spectacle of a lonely Hermit, standing there, waving what may be his last Earthly good-bye among the dreary and arid landscape. The inner, trembling voice wanted to reach out with a verbal last farewell saying:

"Departure!
Oh, do shake my hand, and listen to my song
We know it won't be long before we do the swan
I see the tinge in your eyes, the trailing of sentences, which were once so crisp
We are in a fix to say bye; our hearts cannot be…"

The full twilight shadows cast their eerie light over the humid evening as the revelers settle into their 'preferred spots' to enjoy the coming night's festivities. The rolling waves wash the beach in its foamy sprays as if to calm the previous fire that inhabited the ponds from the hot, midday sun.

Mankin watched as Simnally, dressed in a white shirt and blue pants, moved to what he conceived as a vantage point, on higher ground away from the crowds, to get a quieter view of the beach. This night he was in a quiet mood, and perhaps, was not too keen about poking fun at the new "system," which he sees as a poor substitute for its forerunner. His friend Kenworth opened a huge container with a cold mixture of carrot juice; honey; milk; and a liberal dose of strong, white rum and grated nutmeg. He poured out about a quart and handed it to Simnally, saying, "Simnally, know yourself, man."

Simnally thanked him quietly by nodding his head. He looked steadfastly out on the horizon, sipped his drink then calmly said, "Kenworth, friends like you are what living is all about. Thanks for the carrot juice; it's good," as he lapsed into a reflective stance and quietly focused his eyes on the far horizon. In this contemplative mood he slowly shook his head as if saying no, no, no to some unseen seductive forces that beckon him across space and time.

"Are you OK, Simnally?"

"Yes, I am just thinking about how this festival reminds me about the past Christmas seasons and the antics of Junkunoo bands in the old times during my youth."

"Junkunoo!" exclaimed Kenworth defiantly turning around to face Simnally. "How could anyone with any sense of self-respect like Junkunoo?"

"I didn't say I liked it!"

Kenworth raised his voice and blurted out, "Junkunoo is a demeaning experience, masquerading as an art form. Simnally, which group were you in—the dancers or the observers on the balcony?"

Simnally laughed as he took a sip of his drink, then put his left arm across to his friend's left shoulder and firmly asked, "Which group would you rather be in?"

Mankin closed his eyes and understood the dilemma of second guessing history, especially when one does not have to live it. Yes, most people would rather be in the power group on the balcony than the other performing group where misery manifests itself continually.

"Sometimes, you beat up the Controller Group as if they are all evil, so how come you are now asking which group I would rather be in."

"None of us is totally innocent, even if we called ourselves Pope Innocent. People changed allegiance under torture, whether it is physical or economic. The Controller Group is not the only one to be blamed; the African leaders, then, were also part of the slave trade. They had their political agenda, too. Remember there is a conservative estimate that over 100 million Black Africans were slaves of the Europeans and Arabs, but that is not considered a Holocaust when our slavery was religiously approved by almost all people and their religions."

"Wait! Simnally, you finally see the light that the Catholic Church (Religious Elite), Western Civilization (Capitalistic West) are not the only groups to be blamed for the controlled group's problems. How come no one is beating up the Arabs for their part? Are they not visible?"

"True, but are you going to absolve that spiritless Catholic architect of Black people's disruption, Bartholomew de las Casas, for initiating the 'free market' trip of the Middle Passage? Imagine the Initiator of mass Black debasement trying to use Blacks to exorcise the well-deserved stigma of the 'Black Fame' that is attached to the brutal Spaniards. Spain deserved to be branded as despicable because of its historical cruelty in its treatment to others. Or, are you going to say to the European Jews that building the transport ships were using good business sense, because these ships were noted for their humane and comfortable conditions? Which one of these groups are you apologizing for now, Kenworth? I hope it is not the brutish slave-gathering African chiefs, either. '*Chiefs!*' you know what that means in our everyday language here."

Kenworth nodded his head, made a strong, almost defiant, eye contact with his merry friend, then smile at the word *chief*. He knew that no type of apology from Ghana or any other African state would ever appease most of his friends, who vehemently believed the *chiefs* all knew what they were doing back then. He was mildly surprised that the colloquial usage of the word *chief* is still around. Now, he wonders how and where the word got corrupted in its meaning to such derogatory usage so that it means a simple *village clown*. He wonders if this usage originated with the European conquerors. Quite likely it did; if you were a seller of your own people, selling your own racial group to another powerful racial group, you would be indeed quite simple. It would be just a matter of time before your population declined, and then your individual number would eventually come up, too. No high level of intelligence needed there, just pure and simple common sense. Kenworth took a long satisfying drink then contemplatively murmured: "Imagine a group being oppressed for centuries building ships to transport slaves. They, themselves, eventually had to hide out in the Western World by calling themselves Portuguese. They have the hue; they can hide, but we have no such skin option. Perhaps the whole transporting idea was just a good strategy for their future survival."

Simnally looked squarely in his friend's eyes, and they both laughed aloud.

"The Jews are very good. They are masters of the power game. They helped to enslave them, defended them against slavery, then preached about the virtue of freedom. The full circle, what a group. Plus, as you say, they can hide among their Oppressors if there is a problem. Often times, they are also the Oppressors' policy makers, although that type of popularity works against them."

Both friends laughed in tandem.
"Agreed, Simnally, because the defender for Marcus Garvey was a Jew."

"He was good, as usual. Isn't it funny that the man was trying to take people the other way, by ship, when he was convicted."

"Yes, a non-Jewish-owned ship, too. That is important," remarked Simnally.

"But, the Jews got a piece of the pie in both transactions, though," mentioned Kenworth.

"Kenworth, you noticed that, too; we have many good things to learn from them."

"Like what?"

"...come on, now! You know about many positive things: knowledge of economical power, family solidarity, wisdom of government in a powerful homeland... Now, they finally have a country. Their Holocaust was a sad affair, because the world heard their scream but refused to help. It is hard to believe that this was not a tacit, global agreement to exterminate them. Kenworth do you ever seriously wonder who would be next? Their knowledge of using power is better than most living groups. They survived for a millennium under intense hardship. I have a question for you, Kenworth. Think you can explain to me why Aaron and Miriam were upset with Moses when he married the Ethiopian woman. Was it a loss of power, for them, over Moses? Could it be racism, meaning the Hebrews were of a different color? Or perhaps just plain religious differences, meaning the woman was considered a Pagan? ...think she was Levite, because their priests must marry Levites?"

"She was an outsider, so it may be power. Her color or purity of religion could be a factor, but the end result is power."

"Everything is wanting control, Kenworth, so power it is. Yes, we can learn so much from them."

"How about survival, Simnally?"

Simnally looked at his friend shouting, "Are you mad? We are the survivors of this universe. No one survives as much as we; now, we need to start living as everyone else."

"True. All the media are constantly showing our group as being "the disadvantaged" whenever they choose to depict hardship."

"Kenworth, you believed in Malcolm's doctrine on economic strength, but the man, Garvey, preached that there can be no freedom for our group within the Western World."

"True, Simnally!"

"The man preached spiritual awakening, which can only come through economic strength. We really need to take pride in our race and begin by taking a stand, especially by teaching the young ones some profound social values."

Kenworth looked across the beach in a pensive mood, nodding his head at various angles as he listened to his friend touching on important historical points. He then silently muttered the old Garveyite slogan: "One God! One Aim! One Destiny!"

"The newsmongers claimed an American group planned a "march" to seek some justice."

"No, Kenworth! No! No! Seek justice from whom? This is not the time of MLK. This is a different time, when we have to think about building a nation and have our own economy. Move away from them 'Backra-dependency,' man. We can't keep on living on the other races' charitable attitudes. That type of mental attitude must end."

Kenworth put his clasped hands over his head, then shouted, "Simnally, you have started sounding like Malcolm X, now."

"Malcolm went to Africa, and returned, changed for the better. Garvey wanted us to go to see Africa that we could remain forever changed for the better. Garvey believed in pride, happiness, and nationhood for his people. Give Malcolm credit for some of that, too."

"Simnally, you are right, but there are those in the Americas who believed that his dislike for the NAACP, and other integrationist institutions, was his downfall."

"Kenworth, let's look at the makings of these organizations in their infancy; they were run by intellectuals for various reasons. Some good things came out of them; others, well, not so good. Garvey was not concerned about 'step-function' to partial freedom. He was talking about freedom from the oppressors in totality. He was saying master and slave would not coexist in the same house within this new emancipated paradigm, as most of the abolitionists contrived. Do you think he was wrong, Kenworth?"

"True, Simnally, but you think he was right when he made statement like— 'I **believe in racial purity**... I am proud I am a Negro.'? Don't it sound Hitlerian to you? Next thing you know the man is talking to some Grand Wizard, the bogeyman of his people. Discuss that with me this day, my friend Simnally. What would you say about such a man?"

"Which one you don't believe in, Kenworth? Purity or the other one? They believed in their own purity, so why shouldn't we?"

"Is that a good reason Simnally?"

"Can you think of another, better, reason? You are one of those behaving as though the Black group is a dumping ground for the other races' cast-off. Still receptive to mongrelization Kenworth! Now, you are even finding white, blue-eyed, Asiatic people claiming to be Black because the Oppressor group disallowed them whiteness. This is not being anti-Asiatic either, because the pro-Japanese movement with its Filipino leader did contact Garvey in the 30s. Is black not a color? If so, then let's keep it so and not as a dumping ground for other people's waste."

"That was, then, a Japanese inspired motion in the Eastern World—just their political tactics to offset the USA racial policies. Their present racial attitude shows no such understanding!" emphasized an irate Kenworth.

The discussion had taken a sensitive turn between friends, who for many years had traveled together and had many different views on political and other social problems affecting their race but there was never any doubt that Marcus Mosiah Garvey was the ultimate voice for Black people's freedom. Mankin noticed that Kenworth used the term, "discuss with me this day, my friend Simnally." He was telling the older man that it was not an attack on their beliefs but more of a philosophical discussion to see if they both have the same political awareness. Then there was silence. Simnally took a long drink from his jug, then slowly moved his body into a more comfortable position. Kenworth fixed his eyes on his drink, and tactfully played at removing an imaginary piece of debris from his cup, as the sun slowly set in the distance. Simnally broke the edgy silence by complimented his friend on the quality of their drink. He then smiled and pleasantly asked, "So what you think?"

"About what?" Kenworth asked in a low quiet voice that was meant to minimize any conflict that may have arisen from his last question.

Simnally laughed aloud in a happy voice and shouted, "Kenworth let's have another drink, then perhaps I will answer your little, silly-ass question."

"You have an answer, then, Simnally. Good. I was afraid I would have to answer it for you."

"Kenworth, I am aware you know the answer, but you wanted us to go over the racial politics again to reinforce your belief. When Garvey spoke against the NAACP and the other organizations, they were generally controlled by racially mixed people that were then referred to as mulattos—white intellectuals and their minions who helped the people. But Garvey's true agenda for his followers was total freedom from all the other races, and their sub-groups with their political affiliations, which historically oppressed his people. Garvey was right to be suspicious of them. There were some tactical errors with that Wizard guy, but we all have made mistake as you know by now, right? And, even in that he was not too wrong, because he wanted to show that the people represented by the majority meant to brutally disenfranchise them. He meant to show them what they were up against. He did showed them, too... Yes, he did call Selassie a coward, for losing the war to the Italians. Your Hitlerian suggestion comes from the rumor that he likes Hitler. He likes the German people's economic recovery and strength to reorganize their country after World War 1 when they were up against Western economic shackle. His respect for the Germans was purely on their cohesive ability to recover from a bad situation. Remember they were of the brotherhood of the Slavers. He wished the Black race could have such recovery. Garvey nationalism was in preparedness, Black pride, economic power, and military defense. He wanted a strong Black nation in Africa! The Oppressed Group, sometimes, was their worst enemy. They easily forgot who their enemies were. So they continued repeating the lessons of hardship. Always liking music/dance/and trivial pursuits of styles without substance."

"Is this a European, supremacist idea being used here? The blaming of the Slaves for slavery, Simnally?"

"They were not too blameless, you know, Kenworth. Many were sellers of their own people before they themselves were trapped in bondage when stocks became scarce. One reason why Marcus Garvey had little respect for Selassie was because slavery was still in Ethiopia, and Selassie was also a pawn of the Italians!"

"...like Idi Amin was a pawn of the British MI5 before he choose to think independently, Simnally. How come Garvey blamed Selassie for losing the war in Ethiopia, when he first praised him for taking a stand against Italy? Was he a turncoat when things went wrong?"

"No he blamed him because he continued the trend of the Oppressed Group, always losing to the Oppressor Group. He did not well prepare his people for the fight. Remember, Emperor Menelik defeated the Italians in 1896 **at the battle** near Aduwa. Selassie knew they were his enemies. During that period, all the European nations were carving up Africa. He should have been better prepared to fight. Then he ran away to his European 'friends,' specifically the British. These were the same people most responsible for slicing up Africa into colonial spheres. Eventually, you see what happens; the British accepted Italy's claim to Ethiopia. It was not until the Italians joined the Germans that the British made an attempt to help

Selassie fight to retain Ethiopia's autonomy. The British were not doing Selassie any favor. He even put his trust in the League of Nations, which was an organization of the Oppressor group. Now, who is the coward?"

"The man chose a strategy to win, Simnally!"

"Run-away and win! You think this is the Olympics? Anyway, I will give you this one this time. But take a notice here that the Oppressed Group is always running to the Controller Group, begging for something. Whether it's corporate donation, weapon, food, or otherwise."

"But, the strong should help the weak."

"Two millennium of weakness—is that long enough for you, my excessively patient Kenworth? You noticed that the NAACP is still seeking donations from corporations. There are over 30 million of us, and they still have to seek money from the Controller Group! Anyone controlling your finances will control you."

"True, Simnally, because those groups are still controlled by big corporate donations. It's shameful to see their effectiveness compromised by not having an operational budget to carry on the fight. Those who fund you will always dictate your policies."

"Simnally, I am glad we decided to do something on this island. Man, we will do well too…"

"Yesterday, I went to look at the prison where Garvey was warehoused. They killed many people there, but their collusion could not deter the doctrine of truth. Garvey lives!"

"I visited the courthouse, too. Or, what was left of it."

"Kenworth, in all seriousness, have you ever contemplated that Garvey's prediction came true? If we do not build a powerful nation in Africa, the Black race will never have the respect of the other races in this world."

"A most important point, Simnally. A powerful and respected home of our own."

The two slightly inebriated friends got up simultaneously and brushed the sand from their clothes. They stretched themselves, almost ritualistically, looked over the beach, and shouted over the din of revelers, "Marcus Garvey lives!"

There was a gradual decrease in the sound intensity coming from the beach. People, trying to understand what was going on, silently turned and looked at the two friends on the embankment. Simnally looked at his smiling friend in the **fading twilight** and shook his head with reverence, as if remembering the impressive exploits of his long-past ancestors. In the dimness, he firmly grasped his friends left hand with his right; the two men lifted their arms up high and shouted at the top of their voices, "Power to Malcolm X!"

Kenworth instantly realized that they were true friends, and they have finally reached home. He reached for his friend's mug and drained the last drop of drink into it, politely returned it to Simnally, then moved closer to the embankment. In gusto, he shouted down the beach, "Marcus Garvey lives!"

"Power to sounds and movements, I!" shouted a strong voice from the darkness.

"Marcus Garvey lives!" reflected Mankin in the cool night air as he watched the two friends finally smile with contentment and descend to the beach to the adulation and observation of the would-be revelers. He understood the political dilemma faced by Marcus Garvey in trying to motivate the downtrodden to respect themselves and find a new nation. His problems could parallel the trials of Moses coming out of the biblical Egypt. The Hebrews were physically out of Egypt, but the Egyptian ways were still psychologically imprinted on their minds. It would appear that the Oppressed Group is still begging for acceptance to the entrenched economic and psychological castles of the Controller Group.

When Garvey denounced the NAACP, saying, "...wants us to become whites by amalgamation, but they are not honest enough to come out with the truth."

He was referring to the so-called integration of the races. Mankin wished to take nothing from the respectable and honored NAACP, but during those early years, if your skin was jet black, whom would you trust.? Certainly not the hands that had recently commanded the brutal whippings, nor the deceptive Hybrid class that found your black color so detestable when it suited them. Now, these were the two prominent types within the NAACP. As one looked at the scars and mutilation on black, broken bodies, would you trust their doctrine of telling you to live with each other in peace? Garvey correctly equated both groups as the same people with different agenda. In the Caribbean it was even worst because the Hybrids were even more rabidly racial, even until this day. Surprise! During those times the lines were not as well defined as they are today. The Hybrids struggled to replace their purist European masters as the dominant class. In doing so, they drew a strong racial line against jet-black skinned people. Were they not the ones who excluded the educated and well-deserving people of the Oppressed group from commercial banking jobs right up to the late 1950s and early 1960s in the Caribbean. Can you remember their names? Mankin still remembered the banking industry (Bank of Nova Scotia, Barclay's Bank, Royal Bank of Canada, etc.) which refused to hire highly qualified people of dark skin. The group behind the anti-hiring campaign was made up of people of lighter hue. They were the new power brokers, which were then saddling up to replace their transitional Colonial Masters. Can any person of these institutions now dare to deny this?

Mankin watched the two friends' battle over time with diverse political views. Some of Simnally's views were sometimes quite radical, not amusing but truthful.

Kenworth seemed to be more compromising and apologetic. Perhaps his youth and religious background caused him to be less uncompromising as the old stalwart that faced the enemy, defined it, and refused to be compromised. It is well known that Marcus Garvey and the UNIA were for nation building, but not for the building of Western institutions, because they were not helpful to Black people's happiness. He was very mistrustful of the mixed race especially of their ability to gain the confidence of the Oppressed group. Throughout history they used this information in destroying the progress of the **Oppressed group,** by passing on this information to the white power structure that they admired and wished to be accepted by. No wonder he was against mulattos, because Blacks could not get their rights in the USA or in the Caribbean. He pejoratively referred to them as, "...miscegenation of the race, and their associates, the hybrids of the Negro race."

This was his way of saying we have no power in any group where color is the only dominant imperative. Is this criterion not relevant today?

The UNIA agenda was economic power, integrity of the black race, and Black Nationalism. There was antagonism between American born Blacks and the Black Caribbean immigrants during Marcus' time. The antagonism was not built on the hatred of each other. It was the pompous attitude of the Caribbean immigrants, which upset the Americans. The latter also believed that Garvey's movements were just "bush league" relative to their entrenched church congregations, which were definitely more apolitical. Garvey's approach to racial iniquity was definitely more radical. Even now, compare the hardcore Caribbean political reggae lyrics with the smooth love ballads of their American counterparts, which persisted until the radical "Urban Rappers" come on the scene. Whereas the Caribbean Reggae giants' messages were generally a hammer to "beat down Babylon!" North Americans sing about "...my woman (or man) walked out on me..." Nothing wrong about that either; we all have problems. Some bigger than others though.

Many Americans at first did not give credence to Garvey's doctrine, they still admired him for the respect he demanded and instilled in his followers. Although many people at that time think that Garvey's Back-to-Africa movement was a farce, many of them were not consciously strong enough to come out and say so. One could not, at this time, believe many Caribbean people of mixed heritage would want to join this movement; they were afraid to break ranks to do so. First, they were not economically disadvantaged in their own country. They were generally the oppressors of people with black complexion. Check the records in these islands. Garvey was found guilty of mail fraud in the USA from the irregularities of the Black Star Line stock in1923. He was sentenced to 5 years in prison. Imagine a person of his hue setting up a corporation to repatriate the offspring of slaves. How would the great Western Hemispheres do without their cheap labor? This action certainly would stultify the growth of many powerful and emerging countries. On the other hand, the removal of the Black race would have caused serious consternation among the Oppressor Group. Who would they find as a consensus to hate! They would have to regenerate a dysfunctional pecking list within their own group. Such a system could result in a Middle Eastern-like warring crisis among people with similar views. People are still wondering about Garvey's conviction. Many Island people are still upset about a movement to seek a pardon for Garvey. Every Rastafarian 'Dread I' voiced the opinion that, "The man did nothing wrong... To seek a pardon is saying the man was guilty of something...!" As one 'Bald Head' so accurately put it, "...there are (or were) those among us who still claim **Jesus the Christ** was guilty because man had made a record-keeping system that said so." This brings up the point: How many crimes are committed by "The Ruling Group" and are blamed on the poor and unfortunate people of a specific hue? Political justice seems to dictate, "Leave no loose ends...close the book by putting *them* in the noose!" Most times *they* got away because the poor generally are voiceless and without a face, and the Powerful have no vision or ears to detect anguish incarcerated screams. Can we now understand when the Jews said, "Never Again!"?

Garvey was tried just before the depression. Now, one may ask, were they trying to deflect attention from the impending world economic disaster? Or, is it the continuation of destroying the Black leadership and letting them continue wishing and noisily praying for a coming

Messiah? With this Messiah point in mind, it is easy to understand Simnally's response to taking the non-Messiah route to freedom. During Garvey's incarceration, internecine feuds and assassinations of some his rivals wracked the **UNIA movement**. Was there a powerful voice in Africa that could speak for the Blacks? Africa? No? There wasn't then, and there isn't now, after all these years! To make matter worse, in 1924, the Liberian government even rejected UNIA migration plan to Africa. Garvey was deported to Jamaica in 1925 where there were many obstacles to his aspirations...the zenith of Black international consciousness. This, one can expect from the British Colonial government and their ruling racist buffered mixed-groups. They convicted him of contempt of court in 1929, after he criticized a judge's decision on a Kingston Municipal election result. He called them corrupt! He apologized, but the draconian judge gave him three months in the Spanish Town District Prison.

Practice what you preach! Garvey did. He grew up in a world in the Caribbean where skin color was the predominant key to getting ahead. A place where racism was defined very differently than in the USA. All people with jet-black skin were at the bottom of the heap. All those above were Mixed people (Garvey's Hybrid) of the privileged group who aspired to be like their condescending British overlord. Here the aspiring Hybrids would sell their soul for acceptance to the British circle. There are many horror stories to this effect. Anyway, the staid British usually invited them to parties and rejected the ones they believe had the "tar brush," according to their old sayings. How did they do it? By observing the fluidity of the dancers' movements. If a person's movements were too fluid, then he or she had too many unwanted genes and would not have been invited to their parties. The person was "brushed" off. The common saying was that to get ahead, all polished dancers deliberately stumbled under a Briton's scrutiny. Games people play… Now, do not feel too sorry for these "aspiring" would-be British, because they practiced this type of social exclusion towards the less fortunate black-skinned people. Garvey came from this type of society where opportunities were limited, and the "buffer" group gave no quarters to jet-black skins.

In the 1930s, the world was in a flux. Disadvantaged people were seeking a solace from oppression and economic serfdom. Garvey's UNIA movement made a great impression on many disfranchised people of various background. There were groups from the Pacific who tried courting Garvey's acceptance. These groups insinuated the Japanese were pro-Black as opposed to the USA and other European countries. Some members of the UNIA in Harlem even joined the Communist Party, searching for a home. Garvey admired the political strength and productivity of Hitler until 1942! He wished his people could rise from the ashes and achieve international respect. One has to understand that his downtrodden people were looking for respect from any source. It is similar to the Black African guerrilla movements in the 50s/60s, seeking arms to fight their Western oppressors. The Controller Groups with different political ideology (the USSR communism or Western capitalism) but similar hue is now believed to have made deals to deny the fighters weapons to throw off the yoke of white colonial oppression. One has to ask if there is a global strategy by a *certain* racial group to contain and control people of a *specific* hue. Imagine the intense Cold War conflict between these two political ideologies; neither was willing to sell arms to the struggling Africans until the Chinese arrived on the scene! Of course, we would not expect the West to openly help the Africans march to freedom, because they were the Oppressors, but we would expect the term 'the enemy of my enemy could be a friend of mine' to apply to the USSR.

Some of us perhaps cannot, at this time, ever imagine what legislated exclusion and brutality is like. Garvey, and most people of his hue, experienced it. During this period, many people left the UNIA to join other budding organizations like **Father Divine's PEACE Movement,** diverse black awareness groups, and various religious movements. People were searching for economic power, social justice, self-respect, and inner spirituality. Garvey denounced many of these movements as religious extremists with a lack of vision for the future advancement of the Blacks. In his pragmatism he may have seen many of these Black religious groups as the now famous saying "promising pie in the sky." Garvey believed in religion, but he was a pragmatist who had seen the benefits of effective physical planning. He did not believe the progress of his people should be dependent on the sympathy of the other races that for centuries had oppressed them. For centuries, others race and nations had shown no such disposition of human kindness, why should they start now? Could it also be that Garvey thought religions were too often used to soothe the disadvantaged to accept their contrived stations of inferiority? Remember there were churches that were rabidly anti-Garvey's color. The joke among Caribbean islands people is that the exclusionary **Mormon Church** is now in their islands seeking to *convert them*! The population of these islands mostly is Blacks. Now, who is doing the acceptance here the Organization or the Oppressed? Is this a spiritual or an economical decision to accept Black people in their organization? Mankin pondered if North American integration laws have put the Black population in the mainstream with more dollars to spend. The once despised color certainly has not physically changed, so what has physically changed except economics? So as not to be deceived, "Watch and pray, but pass the…!"

During the Ethiopian-Italian war of 1935, Garvey first praised Selassie for his stance against the Aggresssor. But in 1936, he denounced him for fleeing the country and losing the war. He saw Selassie's flight into exile as an act of cowardice and the loss as a result of his ill preparedness and incompetence. When Selassie appealed to the League of Nations for help, Garvey saw this as just another worthless example of the dependency of the Oppressed Groups on the sympathy of the Oppressors. One can understand why he denounced Selassie. The image for the black skins during those times was one of degenerative incompetence. The image of the smiling, incompetent buffoon as stereotyped by Hollywood and their followers was pervasive. There were no heroes for the people to emulate. And, this was not by chance; it was by design. Not just a Western socio-political design, either. It must have felt great for a disadvantaged group to see their "adopted" brethren (sisters, too) fighting against one of the Beasts of Freedom. Ethiopia was, then, the only African country that had never been conquered by the white man. Now, it was been subdued. It must also be remembered that there was slavery in Ethiopia during this period, and Garvey definitely detested slave states. Ethiopian slavery was abolished in 1942, the year after Selassie returned from exile. Before Haile Selassie 1 (His former name was **Ras Tafari** Makonnen.) was crowned in 1930, he was in bed with the Italians before their invasion of Ethiopia. Oh, please, don't say, "if you can't beat them join them"! When he refused to be their puppet, as was expected, they invaded Ethiopia. Remember Idi Amin and the British (MI5, CIA whatever)? Does this remind you of the continuance of coups against legal governments that are inspired by the more powerful Overlord countries?

Selassie visited Jamaica in 1966.

When Garvey returned home to Jamaica, the UNIA was wracked with dissension and defections. Some of his most famous lieutenants were in open feud with him and with each other. Mismanagement, litigation, government covert meddling, and downright jealousy among its officers destroyed the unity that Garvey had worked so hard to build. At this time, Garvey adopted a new strategy to encompass all groups, including those with different pigmentation. He redefined his strategy to involve some of the more economically advantaged classes. He bought a house, called "Somali Court," in an upscale neighborhood near King's House, where the white and hybrid power groups reside. He started preaching about the advantage of British citizenship and began using the British anthem before each UNIA meeting. It seems his strategy was to deflect the enormous economic pressure that had been intensely directed against the UNIA from the American and European powers. (The "Old Lion" knew he had to make some concessions to the powerful World Rulers for the greater good. One sees similarity with American Black Panther leadership coming home from self-imposed exile. Home is home, and Garvey felt Africa was home.) He also changed the UNIA power structure to reflect a more consensus similar to the middle-class Hybrids of the American society. Garvey made an economical move to the United Kingdom in 1935. He died in London on June 10, 1940.

Bear in mind that the Honorable Marcus Garvey also knew that not all Blacks were suited for returning to Africa. Mankin knows that the dominant doctrinaires of the **UNIA** are no longer as vibrant today, but the doctrine is as relevant today as the air we breathe. The beliefs and awareness of the white Hybrids and Black groups are as vivid as the day Marcus wrote his words. The Oppressor group still rules. The Hybrid groups are still striving to be accepted, although their economic strangle-hold is fiercely felt on the Caribbean islands where they still perpetuate a legacy of hatred and mistrust. The Black group continues to struggle at the bottom of the heap; perhaps, they even aspire to build a nation someplace. Now, they are masters of their political destiny through the polls, but still, are servants of the other two powerful economic groups. "They who have the gold make the rule!"

Let it be remembered that many prominent persons and groups were against Garvey. **The brilliant American Hybrid intellectual W.E. B. du Bois,** and the enigmatic and brilliant poet **Claude McKay** (the Harlem Renaissance Man) had sided with the NAACP. The internal politics of the oppressed or emerging Blacks can be puzzling to us now, especially when one remembers that both Garvey and McKay were from the same island with possible similar shades of black color. Is the color relevant? But of course! Were they from the same Parish? It was felt, then and even now, that Africa was a land of primitive cannibals who contributed nothing to civilization. There are still many people, even within the Black population, who questioned, **"What** have the Africans produced, developed, or designed over the last century?"

Someone asked if supplying the working-class people for Western labor force is considered as a positive contribution. Well?

In other words you may end up in someone's pot if you live in Africa! This was what Garvey was fighting against. Many reasoned they would prefer to suffer slavery than ended up being in someone's stew. Is there some reference in the Christian Bible to the Hebrews' discontent in the wilderness and their preference to be left in Egyptian slavery? Even now the question still remains, "Can anything good comes out of Africa?" This question, planted in slavery, is still being nourished by Blacks all over the world, especially by the Africans, who helped perpetuate the statement by their continual, nefarious wars on each other.

The old rationale that the Europeans caused these wars when they changed tribal boundaries into one country by putting old enemies together during Europe's colonial expansion in Africa cannot be accepted here. The Africans must, now, accept the responsibility for their recent actions and stop blaming the other groups.

With these points in mind, one has to understand the pervasive feeling of uncertainty which permeate the Western psyche during Mackay's time. Giving the limited access to information during those carefree days, would you blame him? One must remember that to Blacks, the immigrants are generally just as mistrustful as they are today. Just remember that being Black in the States is not the same as being Black in other countries. Being Black in the Diaspora and in Africa means strictly color appearance, whereas in the US it means genealogy of the parents. If one is stratified along color lines; then let it be defined by color not by generation. Perhaps Black people in these countries still remember the "house **slaves,**" hence the 1960s sayings, "when the revolution comes and you are not with us (looks like us) then run for cover now."

This is a very misleading statement because one's worst enemy can be your own race. Ask people living in the ghettoes. "Black-on-black" crime is a term used to show the tremendous hatred that seems to permeate the Oppressed group. "Eh, brother give me what you have!" This is not a brotherly request for a "high five" either. Eeek, a gun! Ask the freedom fighters in the South African ghettoes about racial brothers betraying each other. Or, ask those being "necklaced" about their deeds.

Undoubtedly, Claude McKay was a brilliant poet, although many think he showed poor judgment when he did not throw his weight behind Garvey. We all have our own agenda, don't we? This is the man who wrote the poem "If We Must Die" that the arch Briton, Winston Churchill, is supposed to have read to motivate the British troops. 'Roll over Tennyson' (no, not Beethoven.)...

Indeed he may have been able to help and sustain a mass movement the other way to Africa across the Oceans. Mankin wondered what the Oppressor group would do, seeing that they had (still have) an economic axe to grind. Do you think they would kill them all? No! Don't bet on that, it may be more economically feasible to commit another genocide than let them go. Yes, like the biblical Pharaoh trying to "stop them" at the River Jordan before they passed-over... But remember what Claude McKay said:

"...if we must die, let it not be like hogs
if we must die, O let us nobly die.
Like men we will face the murderous, cowardly pack
Pressed to the wall, dying, but fighting back!"

Mankin got caught up in the intensity of the friendly discussion on his "walk throughout time." Now, he wondered how far Garvey was off base when he made some of his statements. Now, if you think about it, we have the benefits of hindsight. One has to be very closed-minded not to understand the dilemma he was up against. There was a tremendous quantity of energy thrown against him from the Overlords, the Hybrids, and his own Oppressed group. Did someone say something about, "man to man is so unjust, you don't know who to trust." What do you believe the immigrants currently think (about this)? Or, do they think! Or, do they ever hear about these episodes? We all know the British are masters of hiding information from conquered people, so perhaps not most immigrants have never heard of the ideas of Marcus Mosiah Garvey. It is a known fact that Blacks are considered reactionary, even in their own groups, if they should speak out about injustice or the "slavery thing." The "other groups" usually use the term "they have an attitude," when the Oppressed group speaks of a grievance. When one of theirs speaks out, it is called a "disagreement." Perhaps this is so because the Oppressed Group has no powerful international ally—we just survive on others sympathy.

It is good to know someone still remembers. Thank you, Simnally, the "Strokes!"

Mankin knows that in life there is absolutely no absolutes; one has to be balanced...don't go too far left, or you may not be in the right, or don't go too far right or you may be wrong. (Or, if you prefer you may also not be right.) Therefore, one has to find a common ground in dealing with all our human problems. One has to take a balanced view that numerous parameters affect the migrant future growth other than the racial issues...and if race is the defining criterion, then where do we go from here? No, do not get too simplistic, here, now...*bleach is not an option*!

As the sun sinks lower into the western sky, casting numerous shadows and colors on the sandy beach...the fading light...gradually changes into a creeping blackness like a blanket obscuring death. Do we now forget the tutelage—the memory—of those who long ago who raised the consciousness of the disadvantaged, who reminded us of the pitfalls that could affect our lives...telling us that some of the dark, damped, and inhumane underground "Slave Pits in Africa" are child's play to those awaiting careless immigrants in the often-bantered present-day free-market society. We have to be contained in the field of opposites. As we watch the sun move away into the shadows, we dare not forget its light...if we do, then darkness (misery and finally a horrifying death) is our lot.

The question now is, "What has happened lately to disprove Garvey's views? One has to ask if the African society has improved relative to China, Israel, and the other emerging countries? Yes, we all know about Liberia and the upheavals in Africa! Yes, the same Liberia that refused Garvey's UNIA migration. The question is still being asked again, and without assessing blame; "Was Garvey correct in his assessment of the progress of the international acceptance of Blacks in the international brotherhood of humans if a powerful Black Nation is not developed in Africa to speak for his race?"

As Mankin watched, the two friends moved down the embankment to the sandy beach. He listened to the sea breeze humming through the trees and watched the continuous wave motion caressing the warm sandy beach. He silently asked Mother Time how many of these discussions she had witnessed at this same spot. He had not really expected an answer, because his senses would not be able to comprehend it. Now, Mankin wondered what had really changed except our perception of reality. Did someone ask, "Are you still in chains?" What? What type...we do make our own chains—imaginary or real—but the effects may be just as physical.

Speaking about chains, it seems as if the British system usually devised a way to reward colonial political winners by putting them in prison first then letting them rule. Remember in the 1950s and 1960s when the old type of Colonialism was on the wane? Most of the newly elected colonial Chief Ministers, Prime Ministers, or whatever they generally called themselves those days, had to get a prison post graduate sentence before being accepted into nationhood. Is this a way of saying; "…we the British Empire are still the boss. Now, have your dinner, and behave, ol' boy." Anyone here remember Jomo Kenyatta in the 1950s or Kwame Nkrumah? Perhaps imprisonment, then, was a signal that you are doing justice for the people. The cruel treatment of Mandela, although not directly attributed to the British, is another case in mind. As a matter of fact, this is a worst-case condition that needed to be remembered. The British and their conniving White Power friends voted against these people in the UN Security Council. Is this the action of friendship? Those were not even the days when they had tusks…did someone of their ilk once called them a toothless Bull Dog? Anyway, we can't just walk away and let sleeping dogs sleep. Someone has to remember! Has anyone remembered dear old Simon for his effort? No, no, not Simon Peter, the Christian disciple. He is remembered by almost everyone. And, not just for the big-time denial or his Earthly defense of cutting off a Roman enforcer's ear.

Someone else wrote, "Crucify Him!" —possible the cry of the entire world while pointing to the powerless Blacks. Is this a reminder of **Simon the Cyrenian,** helping Jesus the Christ with the cross up the heights of Calvary? It would appear the Oppressed Group is deemed to be used, but not to be glorified for their efforts. Has anyone noticed that every race **or** group except ONE is being compensated for crimes committed against them whether in global wars or otherwise. The only group, which had 100 percent slavery, is never compensated. To make matters worse, the Slavers were compensated instead! Imagine getting paid for enslaving others! This free market system is just too complex to unravel... Upturns, downturns, transitional zones! Ever think all these ex-*perts* are just fishing for perks?

PORT MARIA & END OF ISLAND TRIP

A fisherman gathered his thoughts and sat quietly, gazing out on the sea. He noticed ripples where sandy beaches encircled a small islet in the blue-green body of salty water. His knowledge of the sea was astounding...his respect for the sea was high... "...the sea is dangerous but not an enemy..." He was very apolitical as he talked about his local area, the environment, his failed business, and the fulfillment of Marcus Garvey's prophecy. Unbelievable, even the notorious "Bag a Wire" got mentioned, although the fisherman had never once behold the pariah of Garvey's prophecy...

Mankin remembered the man who was supposed to have helped betray the great Garvey. If this in truth was the man, then misery was truly his lot during the latter part of his life! As Mankin watched the knowledgeable fisherman explain fishing techniques and boat design specifications, he understood why the home countries of most immigrant are so poor. These countries have too many of their brilliant people fall through the crack. There is no one to give a helping hand in developing their talents. So many potential rocket scientists are here, eking out a livelihood by fishing in a canoe—a national disgrace and racial tragedy.

On this quiet beach, there are lovers of many ages, in many form of quiet embrace. If you have ever been on a similar beach before, then you have no problem in understanding the meaning of, **"Whet your beak?"** A sensuous command to explore the abundance of riches being offered. An invitation, to resurrect old desires in a sometimes-careless fashion. On the beach, someone asked, "How could you come here without whetting your beak?" If you are not very limp or wet behind the ears, you know this is a command to recognize the pleasures on a beautiful beach. The acknowledge, the serenity of space and time…with the movements of the waves thundering on the quiet sandy beach, like passionate heartbeats when emotion is responding to receptive changing stimulation. It is comforting to hear the "whoosh" sounds of the coming waves **impacting** the quiet sandy beach, followed by the timely synchronicity of water movements as the waves withdraw from the sand, leaving signatures of impregnated wetness. Then the gathering of momentum in moving away, out to sea, only to repeat the continuous cresting motion in satisfying itself or expiring in its experience of wetting a parched beach. A mental picture emerges of human conformity to natural wonders and obedience to the call of nature, to the Spiritual harmony of life. **One retired** fellow frolicked around by himself in the warm Caribbean Sea. Then, suddenly, beautiful middle-aged men and women and sun-seeking retirees descended on the calm, rural beach like zealots trying to win converts. As the sun began to set, an older, shy lady tactfully asked the frolicking retired fellow if he wanted some companionship. The man nodded his head sheepishly, saying, "That may be fun." But, his answer was not fast enough. Another hoarse, inebriated, and assured voice shouted, "Have Viagra, will date!"

The quiet lady calmly bowed to the sheepish retiree and calmly walked away to her Viagara proposal. Mankin was mystified. It appeared manners went out the door when scientific coarseness delivered the goods. People are so end-result oriented that human dignity is no longer of any concern. The lonely retiree stood still, looking at the waning sunset, perhaps reminding himself how the old body changes can be confusing as one grows older. Be graceful, Older One. In years gone by, one of Mankin's old mentors pointed out: "When you are young, your body embarrasses you by misbehaving; creating a spectacle in public. Then, when you are older, it embarrasses you again by misbehaving, this time by not behaving in private the way you wanted it not to behave in public when you were younger. The body rules with constant, contrary embarrassing principles…through some type of a delayed involuntary mechanism."

In other words we want to change our involuntary action to voluntary one.

Immigrants have started to see a vast difference between customs officers in North America and those at their place of birth. It would appear all have come to one agreement. The **customs officers in Canada fiercely** check Black citizens, while professionally allowing whites (even non-citizen) to pass unmolested. They even send their Black citizens to immigration to be checked, as if they doubted their authenticity. On at least one occasion, a Black Canadian citizen asked an immigration officer why was he sent to her? She replied, "I do not know!" When the officer and the Black citizen went to question the customs officer, he was absent—conveniently or otherwise. As Mankin viewed the noisy immigrants, with their numerous ethnic foods, he casually watched the expression of disgust on the faces of the gloved-handed customs officers. While standing in this state of bedlam, he felt the strong dislike these restrained officers exhibited for the returning nuisances "alien citizens." Some of the officers were holding their breath. Other's eyes were like slits of cold icicles, as they asked curt questions through clenched jaws (as if restraining a vomit), while manipulating their gloved arms like robotic end-effectors to carefully take the scraps of papers from the returning "undesirables" without actually touching them. Someone asked the question, or more made the statement, "…look at them. They really hate us!" Body language speaks.

In comparing the attitude to former years, it appears the situation here is definitely racist and hostile. Is this a new, deceptive government procedure? What do you think? A little bit of Apartheid South Africa is being practiced by a trusted and formerly friendly nation to the weak. We all know there are problems within the immigrants' rank, but are you just going to try to kill us all to cure it? True, we as a community must try to get rid of our internal problems. We are now seen as the community of purveyor of the cankerous growth of feeble-minded, drug-infested traders... What a pity...a calamity. Who can the underdogs of this world trust anymore? The world has finally ended!

Now, immigrant people are more comfortable with **the American customs officers!** They are still rigid, but less Mickey Mouse. A citizen is a citizen (unlike in Canada where the race of the citizen caused one to be re-evaluated at customs). Here there are certain spot-checks meant to find chemists: "Are you a chemist?" Has the great country moved towards an anti-chemist bias! Laugh. And what is it with this unwilling battalion of sniffing-attack dogs on leashes, acting as if they want to urinate on luggage? Which union do these dogs belong to? They look so unwilling to work at times. They should make up their minds to work, or go on strike. Always going in contrary directions to their handlers' wishes. "Here, this way, "Flossie." This way..." But, Flossie goes the other way, as if she wanted to do her own thing. One can hear Flossie screaming: "Come with me, or unleash me! You silly-ass-trailing biped!"

Now, the **Island customs officers** are noted for their lack of professional understanding: "Where are you staying? How long? Give me the form (no please?). Immigrants believe that strangers are treated better than their own Nationals are. True or false? Is a smile necessary? Not really, because we know it is a cultural thing not to smile, as North Americans and Europeans do. Most countries will say welcome back to their citizens. Perhaps it would be more pleasant to at least answer a simple question about home when asked. We are not all trying to sneak in contraband. We generally want to say hello after a long flight home. Did you know for many of us this is still home? We feel bad hearing tourists remark, "You think they hate us?" Could be you do, but why be so obvious to strangers who quite possible have never hurt you? Why are customs officers asking returning immigrants for immigration forms? Why not customs declaration forms? Make a decision, and change something at least once in your life. One tourist was heard muttering, "Blacks are universally doing poorly, because they do not know how to effectively use institutions." Mankin wondered if the proof is in this "immigration forms pudding." We seem to have problems making any worthwhile changes to outmoded procedures leftover from our Colonial masters, who were, indeed, real thinkers.

One native migrant, returning to school after a year's absence could not find his island immigration papers. As the student fumbled under the unsmiling gaze of the bureaucrat, he intelligently asked why he needed immigration papers when he was not an immigrant. The bureaucrat coldly replied, "You want fi see I nuh make you go no way?" After a while, the testy little bureaucrat finally handed the student his documents mumbling, "…think mi ah any kunu-munoo …anyway, don't go up there and give us any bad name down here, because we are good and decent people. Study hard too…" The student stopped and looked in the officer's face and saw a warm human spirit behind the mundane bureaucratic mask. You never can tell with people, sometimes…so take a chance with your humanity. Mankin agreed there is good in all of us, even people who are employed at Barriers to keep others in. Or is it out?

TIME TO RECONSIDER YOUR LAST WALK

Some one once wrote, "Where will you spend eternity (on earth)?" Then, a funeral home posted the sign: "When the time of life is ended see Uncle Joe!"

Troubling statements, aren't they? Ever think whom Uncle Joe may be...for all eternity? This may be like retirement in a foreign convalescent home, where the politicians keep cutting back on the services while your pain increases. As you look through tired, fading eyes at the plastic flowers**, there passes another** fawning, over-perfumed funeral undertaker to *tak*e another one of your old next-door friends *"under."* You now think that you may have breakfast today and perhaps this evening, or even later tonight you will have a visitor...perhaps a friend from the old country for the very last time! The trend in rapid materialism has led us to this chronic state of individualism, which results in alienation of the migrants' old support groups. This breakdown of their social network caused them to mistrust each other. The result is the greater dependency on technology for individual security and comfort. People, now, believe monitoring devices are helping them to be safe and comfortable. Everyone is too busy to visit sick friends or even older relatives. The new feeling is in keeping with the jaded business slogan, "What have you done for me lately... You can't help me anymore." Watchfulness is in, but it is now done technologically, with a camera to watch sick parents. The children just call institutional "watchers" to satisfy their curiosity (not conscience. They are still working on the conscience part.) They need a conversational piece to tell friends that they keep in touch with mom or "dear old dad." Remember the monitoring camera will show something, but it is not reality. The picture has no sense of atmosphere, tone, the feeling of what happened before, or what went on at the periphery. It is a utilitarian tool for monitoring people. In this type of abstract and utilitarian world, the old migrant spirit sometimes fades faster than butter in the sun. It is a true statement that our family will never remember many of us. Now, we sit and wonder:

Is there any one out there to tell about our lives? Is anyone willing to write about our experiences, our feelings, and us? Who will write our stories?

Certainly the immigrants would have preferred their own people telling their stories, but it seems there is unwillingness within the group to do so. Are they ashamed, lethargic, indolent, or just too busy, being unaware or just plain incapable of realizing what history means to our group? Perhaps the group is heavily populated with procrastinators who have failed to see the importance of today's events. They still believe in tomorrow. Wake up, today is the shaper of the tomorrows. Tomorrow is for the tombs of stillness, as one blissfully doses away in a shroud of mist and then the final darkness where all the essences of life fades into mere fleeting and vanishing memories.

We have nourished others throughout the ages but have never been historically recognized for our labors—not even in today's mega-information society where the media rules with massive doses of information. We have sung many sweet songs although our hearts are heavy with our unfulfilled dreams. Can we rest comfortably and feel good, knowing that we had given our best and that our children will carry on and be much more comfortable than us in our alienated society? Alas, but this does not appear to be so at this time. It appears that our adopted country, with its present mass information technology, is geared to stratify us in an alienated work group of servile peons, whose main function is to keep the law enforcement establishment employed. They give armaments to the conservative politicians and media moguls to fuel their hate mongering speeches and to transportation agencies who transport us en masse to manufacturing areas from our native land.

"This is nothing new," you say.

"Then, are you satisfied with this? Is this what you want to passed on to those whom you profess to love?"

Is this the way the people across the Middle Passage felt when the "grim reaper" came knocking at their doors as they observed their offspring in a strange, hostile, and spiritless environment that they toiled to build? Now, you know how conquered people feel. Comparatively the years are numbered differently from then, but the problem of the human spirit trying to overcome alienation still persists today. Will someone please give us a face, a name, and an agenda? Please! We made contributions to all those worlds but are now locked out—not just by "the glass ceiling" of the business sectors but by those we nourished from infancy. They are still censuring us in their numerous criminally "profiling" ways. Will they ever stop?

Most older immigrants grew heavyhearted with longings for their own people and the camaraderie and conviviality that goes with that type of living. As their sojourn grew longer, they questioned themselves about their future (or lack of it) in their newfound, spiritually unresponsive world. Will they ever be united with those they consider to be their real friends from childhood? Or, is "what they now see, is what it will be forever, amen?" Will they, forever, live this life of mentally wondering about future dreams? Are we home in the future, yet? In their mind's eye, they see themselves being welcomed home with total acceptance and respect. They all want the type of acceptance given older statesman in a new and better world. They all want the knowledge that their children will not be subjected to the alien tests, being considered as social rogues of a sub-species to be labeled an "unwanted underclass," to be contained by the social and cultural provisions of the ruling groups, to be always pigeonholed with the dreaded 'African-X' group label, which defines one as a target for the institutional enforcers... In their native land one would be just another normally named person walking down the street.

Will we ever see our own birth country pass through a positive cycle as we have observed in our adopted countries? Only time will tell. Can we ever solemnly attended the last rites of our dearly departed ones, compatriots, or families without the crushing economic burdens of intercontinental transits and draconian scrutiny of unfeeling security personnel at customs barriers. Will we ever have insight to question, "Who will attend our funeral, when we are so far away."?

As our physical bodies change with age, our spirit looks home to a quieter, gentler (that description again!) place to be, but the industrial worlds are not the optimum place for such condition. The various immigrant groups return, sometimes, not out of shame but out of pain. Others, of course, return through pride, and hopefully the majority return because they have finally come to their senses to know that everything good cannot be found in one geographical locale.

We must enjoy the journey through life, because the fun may be in the travel, not at the destination... Think!

"We shall gather at the river, the beautiful, the beautiful river… Gather we…"

ABOUT THE AUTHOR

Jamaica is my place of birth, but my residence is now California. In the last six years, I have increased my visits to Jamaica to keep in touch with my roots. I planned residing there in a couple years. To that end, I am fine-tuning my relocating plans. There are numerous changes on the island; unfortunately, not all for the best. Not withstanding that, the call of the island is still strong for anyone who is seeking a spiritual solitude from a stress filled and industrial regimented life… I spiritually "see," "hear" and "feel" the warm Caribbean seas with its meandering beaches, and the surrounding lush vegetation calling, "Come home and be revitalized—"

I have written four novels, two of which are science fiction, that I am trying to get published.